Cambridge Elements

PRAGMATISM AND THE ORIGINS OF THE POLICY SCIENCES

Rediscovering Lasswell and the Chicago School

William N. Dunn
University of Pittsburgh

CAMBRIDGE
UNIVERSITY PRESS

University Printing House, Cambridge CB2 8BS, United Kingdom

One Liberty Plaza, 20th Floor, New York, NY 10006, USA

477 Williamstown Road, Port Melbourne, VIC 3207, Australia

314–321, 3rd Floor, Plot 3, Splendor Forum, Jasola District Centre, New Delhi – 110025, India

79 Anson Road, #06–04/06, Singapore 079906

Cambridge University Press is part of the University of Cambridge.

It furthers the University's mission by disseminating knowledge in the pursuit of education, learning, and research at the highest international levels of excellence.

www.cambridge.org
Information on this title: www.cambridge.org/9781108730518
DOI: 10.1017/9781108676540

First published 2019

A catalogue record for this publication is available from the British Library.

ISBN 978-1-108-73051-8 Paperback
ISSN 2398–4058 (online)
ISSN 2514–3565 (print)

Pragmatism and the Origins of the Policy Sciences

Rediscovering Lasswell and the Chicago School

Elements in Public Policy

DOI: 10.1017/9781108676540
First published online: March 2019

William N. Dunn
University of Pittsburgh

Author for correspondence: William N. Dunn, dunn@pitt.edu

Abstract: This Element examines the origins of the policy sciences in the School of Pragmatism at the University of Chicago in the period 1915–1938. Harold D. Lasswell, the principal creator of the policy sciences, based much of his work on the perspectives of public policy of John Dewey and other pragmatists. Characteristics of the policy sciences include orientations that are normative, policy-relevant, contextual, and multidisciplinary. These orientations originate in pragmatist principles of the unity of knowledge and action and functionalist explanations of action by reference to values. These principles are central to the future development of the policy sciences.

Keywords: pragmatism, policy sciences, Harold D. Lasswell, abduction, functionalism

ISBNs: 9781108730518 (PB), 9781108676540 (OC)
ISSNs: 2398–4058 (online), 2514–3565 (print)

Contents

Preface

The policy sciences are in part a continuation of a tradition of policy-relevant social science research that began at the outset of the nineteenth century. It is a misconception, however, that social science research in the nineteenth century determined what became the policy sciences in the next. My own awareness of this misconception came relatively late in my journey through the policy sciences and its several tributaries, including policy studies, policy analysis, and program evaluation. Indeed, only recently did I discover that the policy sciences originated not only in the pioneering contributions of Harold Lasswell, the main founder of the policy sciences, but equally importantly in the policy-oriented approach to social science research of John Dewey and other pragmatists.

The relationship between the policy sciences and pragmatism can be investigated in many ways. In this context, one of Lasswell's main arguments, as it was of James, Peirce, and Dewey, is that social scientists are and should be committed not only to creating knowledge about social problems but also to see that such knowledge contributes to their solution.[1] In response to Robert S. Lynd's rhetorical question, *Knowledge for What?* (1939), pragmatists affirm the centrality of the social and behavioral sciences for understanding and resolving many of the most important social problems.

I proceed from the point of view that the influence of pragmatism on Lasswell and the policy sciences should be taken as an object of inquiry, as a research question, rather than as a forgone conclusion or confirmed hypothesis. Accordingly, the foregoing narrative attempts to provide plausible answers to three main questions:

- Where in Lasswell's writings do we find the influence of William James, Charles Sanders Peirce, John Dewey, and other pragmatists? Answering this question requires a logical, epistemological, and methodological analysis of what Lasswell, his closest colleagues, and students wrote about the relationship between the policy sciences and pragmatism.
- With what pragmatists – individuals as well as members of disciplinary departments and "schools" – did Lasswell interact as a student and then as a faculty member at the University of Chicago (1927–1937) and Yale University (1943–1970)? Answers to this question call for an analysis of the disciplinary matrix of students, colleagues, and academic administrators that enabled and constrained Lasswell's work and that of his main collaborator, Myres S. McDougal.

[1] To quote Lasswell's almost mantra-like maxim, the policy sciences "are concerned with knowledge *of* and *in* the decision processes of the public and civic order" (Lasswell 1971b: 1).

- What implications for the practice of policy research and analysis in universities, governments, and nongovernmental organizations issue from answers to these questions? Here, among other implications, I consider the benefits of discarding misconceived linear and cyclical models of policy making, and replacing them with the model of a complex circuit. The "circuitry" of policy making, rather than the imagery of policy cycles, is more consistent with Lasswell's views. I also suggest that we make an effort to develop a better understanding of policy change by (a) turning to functionalist and teleological theories of the decision process, by (b) moving beyond deduction and induction to the use of abductive reasoning in formulating policy problems, and by (c) exploring John Dewey's variant of pragmatism, which he called instrumentalism, to achieve a greater understanding of and capability to shape the use of scientific evidence in policy making. One benefit of instrumentalism may be the resolution of problems that stem from the associational fallacy of policy relevance: We have tended to view the process of policy analysis as relevant to the process of policy making merely because both processes involve superficially similar functions.

These questions guide this investigation of pragmatism and the origins of the policy sciences.

1 Pragmatism and the Policy Sciences

Harold D. Lasswell and several prominent collaborators, including Myres S. McDougal, Abraham Kaplan, and Daniel Lerner, were the principal creators of the policy sciences.[2] After 1950, Lasswell's new vision of policy-relevant social sciences became a major multidisciplinary movement, one he described in one of his last major works as "a contemporary adaptation of the general approach to public policy recommended by John Dewey and other pragmatists" (1971b: xiii–xiv).

The policy sciences are rooted in the philosophy of pragmatism as it evolved in the hands of William James, Charles Sanders Peirce, and other members of the "metaphysical clubs" that arose in New England in the late 1800s. The master intellectual historian of pragmatism, Louis Menand (2001: 220–221), reminds us that the term *metaphysical*, which actually designated a social group of philosophically minded, intellectually probing professors and

[2] Lasswell's most important collaborator and a virtual cocreator of the policy sciences was Myres S. McDougal. Their magnum opus is *Jurisprudence for a Free Society: Studies in Law, Science, and Policy*, 2 vols. New Haven, CT: Martinus Nijhoff Publishers, 1992. The two volumes document the history of their collaboration on the development of the policy sciences.

lawyers, ironically frowned agnostically upon metaphysics. Peirce, the founder of the first metaphysical club, wrote that all knowledge is social. "[I]n a universe in which events are uncertain and perception is fallible, knowing cannot be a matter of an individual mind 'mirroring' reality . . . Reality doesn't stand still long enough to be accurately mirrored . . . knowledge must therefore be social" (Menand 2001: 200). This perspective, which later became an integral part of John Dewey's social interactionist theory of truth as "warranted assertibility," was a methodological pillar of the Chicago School of Pragmatism and Lasswell's policy sciences.

The policy sciences are based in part on the evolution of problem-oriented empirical research in nineteenth-century Europe, an evolution documented in historical accounts by Lerner (1959) and by Wagner, Weiss, Wittrock, and Wollman (1994/2008). However, few scholars before Lasswell and his colleagues at the University of Chicago combined multidisciplinary breadth with a pragmatic theory of knowledge that saw the social sciences as instruments of policy action.[3] Accordingly, the policy sciences mandated the creation of knowledge about the policy-making process, but required that such knowledge be used to improve that process and its outcomes.

Social Sciences and Modern States, National Experiences and Theoretical Crossroads (Wagner et al. 1994/2008) was the first systematic effort to assess four decades of progress of the policy sciences. Although this important edited volume included historical reviews by contemporary policy science scholars such as Peter DeLeon (1994) (also see DeLeon 1988, 2006), it concluded that the policy sciences were neither new nor unprecedented. After pointing to efforts by Aristotle, Plato, and Machiavelli to provide policy advice to the political leaders of the day (e.g., Aristotle's tutelage of Philip of Macedon), the authors note that in seventeenth- and eighteenth-century Europe, the term *Polizeywissenshaften* was in good currency in German-speaking countries.

In the nineteenth century, statistics and demography developed as specialized fields.[4] The Manchester and London Statistical Societies, established in the 1830s, helped shape a new orientation toward policy-relevant knowledge. The two societies hoped to replace traditional thinking about social problems with empirical analyses of the effects of urbanization and unemployment on the

---

[3] An early predecessor of the policy sciences was Rice and Lasswell's *Methods in the Social Sciences: A Case Book* (1931). The volume grew out of Charles Merriam's efforts, as president of the Social Science Research Council, to integrate the social sciences (Crick 1959: 169–170). Merriam was the head of the political science department at the University of Chicago and Lasswell's academic advisor.

[4] The foregoing discussion draws on chapter 2 of my *Public Policy Analysis: An Integrated Approach*, 6th edn. (New York, NY: Routledge, 2018).

lives of workers and their families. In the Manchester Statistical Society, research was coupled with a commitment to social reform. A preeminent contributor to the methodology of social and economic statistics and survey research was Adolphe Quetelet (1796–1874), a Belgian mathematician and astronomer who was the major scientific advisor to the Dutch and Belgian governments. In the same period, Frederic Le Play (1806–1882) conducted detailed empirical investigations of family income and expenditures of European workers in several countries.

In England, Henry Mayhew and Charles Booth studied the life and employment conditions of the urban poor in natural (what we now call "field") settings. In writing *Life and Labour of the People in London* (1891–1903), Booth employed school inspectors as what today we know as key informants. Using what now we call participant observation, Booth lived among the urban poor, gaining firsthand experience of actual living conditions. A member of the Royal Commission on the Poor Law, he was also an important influence on the revision of policies on old-age pensions. Booth's work served as something of an exemplar for policy-oriented research in the United States, including Jane Addams's *Hull House Maps and Papers* (1895) and W. E. B. Du Bois's *The Philadelphia Negro* (1899). Addams was a colleague, friend, and confidant of John Dewey and George Herbert Mead, who followed Dewey as the most influential pragmatist and social scientist at the University of Chicago. Addams was also the founder of the American Civil Liberties Union (ACLU), the largest advocacy group in the United States committed to the protection of civil liberties.

The rise of empirical and policy-relevant research was not the result of declarations of methodological loyalty to empiricism and the scientific method. Declarations to this effect did not occur until the rise of logical positivism in the next century, when Vienna Circle philosophers engaged in the logical reconstruction of physics and proposed formal principles and rules to guide scientific practice. Instead, the rise of empirical and policy-relevant research originated in the uncertainty accompanying the shift from agrarian to industrial society. Older methods for understanding the natural and social world were no longer adequate. The key questions of the day were practical: How much did members of the urban proletariat need to earn to maintain themselves and their families? What level of earnings was required before there was a taxable surplus? How much did workers have to save to pay for medical treatment and education? How much investment in public works projects – sanitation, sewage, housing, roads – was required to maintain a productive workforce and protect the middle and upper classes from infectious diseases cultivated in urban slums? Policy-oriented empirical research provided answers to these and other questions.

1.1 The Policy Sciences Circa 1930

In the United States, the phrase "policy sciences" was used in a 1943 memorandum by Lasswell titled "Personal Policy Objectives"(Lasswell 1943; cited in Brunner 1991), followed by the edited volume *The Policy Sciences* (Lerner and Lasswell 1951). Apart from publications, however, one of the first uses of the term was in 1932 in a course titled "Policy Sciences" at Yale Law School (Van Doren and Roederer 2012). The course was offered by Thurman Arnold, a professor at Yale Law School, and Edward S. Robinson, a Yale professor of psychology.

The aim of the policy sciences, as understood at the time, was to approach government as a science – as a *policy science*. For Arnold (1937: ii), governments should be studied by scientific observation, not "in the light of faiths and symbols." When in 1937 Arnold became the assistant US attorney general in the Roosevelt administration, the course was taken over by Myres S. McDougal, who became Lasswell's lifetime collaborator. Their thirty-year collaboration is documented in the 1,588-page *Jurisprudence for a Free Society* (1992), a synthesis of their work in developing the policy sciences. At the same time, Arnold's book, *The Folklore of Capitalism* (1937), thanked Lasswell for his assistance. He was the only social scientist among a group of jurists and law professors who, in contrast to Lasswell, were largely unprepared to study political, social, and economic aspects of law.

By 1938, Arnold, McDougal, and Lasswell were colleagues. Ironically, this was the same year that Lasswell, already a well-established scholar whom Almond (1987) later described as a preeminent twentieth-century social scientist, was denied promotion to a full professorship by University of Chicago president Robert Maynard Hutchins (Bulmer 1984: 204; Dzuback 1991: 173). Lasswell subsequently resigned from Chicago, joining McDougal at Yale Law School in 1943, after serving during World War II as chief of the Experimental Division for the Study of Wartime Communications at the US Library of Congress.[5]

1.2 Legal Realism and the Policy Sciences

Legal realism is a philosophy of law that asserts that in seeking explanations of the development of legislative acts and other policies, the investigator should focus, first, on judicial, legislative, and executive decisions, not on legal principles, doctrines, or rules. "The Realists [capitalization original] successfully demonstrated that, by reference to rules alone, neither scholar nor practitioner could explain why past decisions had been made or how future decisions

[5] Harold F. Gosnell, a political scientist who conducted studies of Negro (African-American) and machine politics in Chicago, resigned for the same reason in 1942.

were likely to be made" (Reisman 1998: 35). Thurman Arnold and Myres McDougal were leading legal realists of their day, and it was legal realism and not pragmatism per se that motivated the teaching of the policy sciences in 1932–1933 at Yale. However, legal realists "were much less successful in identifying the tasks the jurist [and other policy makers] should perform and the methods to be deployed" (Falk, Higgins, Reisman, and Weston 1998: 729). Hence the need for social science methodologists such as Lasswell.

Arnold and McDougal saw legal realism as practical, but it was not *pragmatic*, in the sense of that term used by Dewey and other pragmatists at Chicago. Judging from Arnold's published disagreements on key pragmatist principles with Sidney Hook, an influential pragmatist philosopher of the time (Arnold 1937: 349–353), Arnold probably was not a pragmatist. As for Lasswell, it is clear from records of his interaction with members of the Chicago School of Pragmatism (1927–1933) that he was influenced by pragmatism when he was an undergraduate, a doctoral student, and then a faculty member at the University of Chicago.

In identifying the methods they should deploy in explaining past decisions, Lasswell and McDougal (1943, 1992) and Lasswell and Kaplan (1950) viewed the development of laws and policies as a process of making authoritative decisions about the achievement of human dignity and values of enlightenment, power, wealth, well-being, affection, respect, rectitude, and skill. To identify the operations required to achieve human dignity and associated values, they identified a sequential but broadly iterative process of decision-making with seven functions: intelligence, promotion, prescription, invocation, application, appraisal, and termination (Lasswell and Kaplan 1950; Lasswell 1956a; McDougal and Lasswell 1967). In this context, scholars and practitioners were seen to share tasks that contribute to what Lasswell and McDougal labelled *intelligence*, which was the sine qua non of performing the remaining six functions. In performing the intelligence function, decision makers:

- Identify problems in achieving goals
- Chart relevant past decisions
- Analyze factors affecting trends in achieving goals
- Forecast likely future conditions
- Identify and assess likely future decisions
- Clarify values and identify alternative solutions.

These tasks, it should be stressed, point toward future decisions, not to present or past ones. Later, in his presidential address to the 1956 meeting of the American Political Science Association, Lasswell emphasized that policy scientists

> should take the lead in integrating rather than dividing our intellectual community. Compared with an entire university, which has become a non-communicating aggregate of experts, each department can become a true center of integration where normative and descriptive frames of reference are simultaneously and continuously applied to the consideration of the policy issues confronting the body politic as a whole over the near, middle, and distant ranges of time. (Lasswell 1956b: 797)

Lasswell's 1956 recommendation is a mirror image of the institutional matrix in which the Chicago School of Pragmatism functioned after 1920.

At Yale Law School, Myres S. McDougal was an eminent scholar of international law, jurisprudence, and public policy. With Lasswell and other colleagues at Yale,[6] McDougal worked for more than thirty years on legal education for public policy, or what we now might describe as professional training in policy analysis.[7] For his part, Lasswell brought to the study of legal realism the perspectives and tools of psychology, sociology, communications, and political science, that is, elements of the multidisciplinary approach to law and public policy of which Lasswell was a master.[8]

In succeeding years, Lasswell was to become one of a handful of creative innovators in the social sciences. Gabriel Almond, one of his most successful Chicago students, has described Lasswell as "the most original and productive political scientist of his time" (Almond 1987: 249).

Lasswell's works ranged from books and articles on propaganda and social communication to political psychology and the policy sciences. Under the umbrella of the policy sciences, Lasswell invented what we know today as the two fields of policy studies and policy analysis, the former situated in the discipline of political science and the latter offered as part of curricula in microeconomics and decision analysis in professional schools of public policy.[9] The body of Lasswell's work in the policy sciences is composed of

---

6 Other Yale collaborators included Arnold Reisman and Richard Falk. See Falk et al. (1998).

7 Prior to the establishment of professional schools of public administration and public policy, professionals trained in law, rather than in applied microeconomics, policy analysis, and public administration, were the largest group of professionals prepared at Yale and other law schools for policy work at the national level.

8 A third important influence, one that is related to Lasswell's pragmatist moorings, was his own experience as a policy practitioner during World War II. As chief of the Experimental Division for the Study of Wartime Communications at the Library of Congress, Lasswell directed policy studies that improved American wartime propaganda and opposed that of Germany and the Nazi war effort, while concurrently validating his functional model of social communication.

9 A wider historical review of antecedents of *policy analysis* would include the rise of management science, operations research, and cost-effectiveness analysis during and immediately after World War II, particularly at the RAND Corporation. By contrast, *policy studies* grew out of political science and public administration in roughly the same period. At that time, RAND and the policy sciences were close. For example, E. S. Quade (1989), a prominent applied mathematician and policy analyst at RAND, was the first editor of the journal *Policy Sciences*.

his singly authored and coauthored contributions with Myres McDougal (Lasswell and McDougal 1992) and Abraham Kaplan (Lasswell and Kaplan 1950/2008). Lasswell and McDougal, after the first general programmatic statement of the scope and methods of the policy sciences by Lerner and Lasswell (1951), were virtual cocreators of the policy sciences, notwithstanding their early collaboration, in 1932–1933, with Thurman Arnold, to establish the initial contours of the policy sciences in their course at Yale. Later, in 1943, Lasswell joined McDougal at Yale (Falk et al. 1998), remaining there for nearly thirty years until moving to Columbia University in 1970.

1.3 The Roots of Pragmatism

Lasswell's relationship with pragmatism has roots in his interaction with pragmatists at the University of Chicago. Ascher and Hirschfelder-Ascher (2004: 7) show how Lasswell's approach to political psychology was affected by Dewey's biologically based functional psychology, years after Dewey had physically relocated to Columbia University in 1904. This same pragmatist commitment to theories of functionalism and instrumentalism underlies Lasswell's well-known maxim (1971b: 3) that the function of the policy sciences is to create knowledge *of* and *in* the policy-making process. Lasswell's policy sciences were a product of various social science "schools" at Chicago, in particular the Chicago School of Pragmatism, which fostered a cohesive network of affiliated colleagues in the social and behavioral sciences.

Regrettably, the relation between pragmatism and the policy sciences has been misunderstood. The policy sciences have been wrongly visualized as the simple application to practical problems of social science theory and methods, for example, the application of microeconomics to problems of choosing alternatives with smaller opportunity costs, as reflected in lower discount rates for future cost and benefit streams. Properly speaking, however, such applications – which environmental economist Daniel Bromley calls the conventional Paretian approach to pseudo-economic choices (Bromley 2006:13–14) – are not examples of pragmatism. The error is in assuming that social sciences such as economics and political science are policy sciences, simply because they deal with potentially applicable practical knowledge, as contrasted with traditional social science disciplines, which deal with intellectual knowledge that is valued primarily for its own sake.

Abraham Kaplan, one of the most respected pragmatists of his generation, observes that pragmatism has been widely misunderstood because concepts such as "practice" and "action" have been understood in a restrictive sense.

"There is a vulgar pragmatism in which 'action' is opposed to 'contemplation,' 'practice' to 'theory,' and 'expediency' to 'principle' ... this vulgar doctrine is almost the direct antithesis of pragmatism, which aims precisely at dissolving all such dualities"(Kaplan 1964: 43–44). In other words, practice is the consummation of theory; theory originates in and guides action. The fusion of the contemplative-theoretical with the practical-contextual is what Lasswell and Kaplan (1950) meant by the term *pragmatic*. Kaplan informs us that:

> action that is relevant to the pragmatic analysis of meaning must be construed in the broadest possible sense, so as to comprise not only the deeds that make up the great world of affairs, but also those that constitute the scientific enterprise ... The "usefulness" that pragmatism associates with truth is as much at home in the laboratory and study as in the shop and factory, if not more so. (Kaplan 1964: 44)

Therefore, pragmatism is not coextensive with the simple application of theories and methods to practical problems. This is evident in the differences among varieties of pragmatist thought (Rescher 1995: 710–713; Menand 2001; Shields 2004). Whereas Peirce was largely an objectivist, holding that multiple theories mirror in different ways socially constructed beliefs about nature, James was a subjectivist, which partly reflected his skepticism about what he saw as the potentially harmful effects of modern science. For James, beliefs may mirror subjective rather than objective states: beliefs may make us feel content, secure, or spiritually worthy, apart from objective external conditions. Dewey and colleagues at Chicago, however, were neither objectivists nor subjectivists; they were transactionists. Beliefs fulfill different ends that are realized and adapted through social interaction (Hickman 2009: 143–162). Rucker sums up the differences between the three men:

> Only at the University of Chicago at the turn of the century did there grow up a school of American philosophy. The pragmatism that John Dewey and his colleagues and students collaborated on there had its roots in James and Peirce, but what emerged from their efforts was distinctively their own ... Neither James's concern to rescue sentiment from what he saw as the onslaught of science nor Peirce's drive to systematize modern thought represented the main thrust of American culture. The Chicago philosophers shared James's practical orientation, in contrast to Peirce's emphasis on theory ... as opposed to James's fear that science, too narrowly interpreted, was a threat to human values. The Chicago pragmatists saw both science and values arising from human action, and they proceeded to derive an entire philosophy from the analysis of action. This action-derived philosophy turned out to be a pragmatism different from both Peirce's logic-centered thought and James's psychology-based work. (Rucker 1969: vi)

Dewey and the Chicago School of Pragmatism had a marked influence on philosophy, psychology, sociology, and political science. The worldview of pragmatism, as Bulmer (1984: 29–32) observes, focused on the process of change and adaptation that affects humans as well as physical objects. Activities such as policy implementation and appraisal, for example, generate actions designed to achieve the goal of human dignity and attendant values such as intelligence, power, wealth, and rectitude. "Ends were seen as relative to the circumstances in which action was undertaken" (Bulmer 1984: 29), circumstances that included the seven functionally defined decision processes elaborated by Lasswell (1956a). Values are not fixed or immutable, but contextual and transactional, arising out of the interaction of groups of persons, not individuals working alone. Base-values (means) and scope-values (ends) are in continuous flux.

1.4 Dewey's Reflex Arc

Interpreters of the policy sciences in Europe and the United States have sometimes conflated pragmatism with acts of being practical. This is perhaps understandable, at least in part, because Lasswell, one of the two principal architects of the policy sciences, wrote sparingly about the link between the policy sciences and pragmatism. Indeed, it was not until 1971 that Lasswell acknowledged that the policy sciences were a product of the ideas of John Dewey and other pragmatists. While John and Alice Dewey left the University of Chicago in 1904, which might suggest that the reign of pragmatism had ended, Dewey's influence on philosophers, psychologists, sociologists, and political scientists prevailed at Chicago well into the late 1930s. Dewey either had brought with him from his last post at the University of Michigan, or later hired, a group of pragmatists that included James R. Angell, Edward S. Ames, George H. Mead, Addison W. Moore, and James H. Tufts. These Chicago professors, and not Dewey alone, were instrumental in establishing the Chicago School of Pragmatism.

1.5 The Reflex Arc and Functionalism

One of Dewey's most widely known and influential papers, one that is acknowledged to capture the essence of his thought, is "The Reflex Arc Concept in Psychology," published in 1896 in *Psychological Review*. The paper, a contribution to philosophical psychology, was a critique and reformulation of principles of adaptive learning proposed by William James in *The Principles of Psychology* (James 1890). Adaptive learning, which today is often represented as one or more *feed-forward* and *feed-back* loops, was an extension of Charles Sander Peirce's "The Fixation of Belief"

(1877).[10] Peirce wrote that the catalyst for adaptive learning is prior doubt, or what today we know as the "surprises," "anomalies," or "indeterminate situations" that policy analysts and policy makers frequently face. Peirce contended that: "Doubt stimulates us to action until [doubt] is destroyed. This reminds us of the irritation of a nerve and the reflex action produced thereby ... The irritation of doubt causes a struggle to attain a state of belief. I shall call this struggle *inquiry*" (Peirce 1877: 13).

Adaptive learning – or the struggle to pass from a state of doubt to beliefs in which we have sufficient confidence to act – was an organic and distinctly human enterprise, not a process of mechanistic stimulus and response.[11] The flame of a candle illustrated the reflex action that follows the stimulation of a nerve. The act of touching the flame was followed by pain and the rapid withdrawal of the hand. The example of this sequence from stimulus to response – from flame to pain to withdrawal – can be traced to Rene Descartes, for whom "an external impulse, say from a burned foot, activates a kind of cord or cable attached to the brain. The brain then activates another cable attached to the foot, thus completing the reflex arc" (Hickman 2009: 7). This mechanistic view was later modified by William James (1890: 526–527), who saw the reflex arc as an extension of several stages and types of stimuli and responses, some objective and some subjective.

In the nineteenth century, an organic theory of the reflex arc – a theory that is humanistic and not mechanistic – was typically illustrated by the image of a child touching a candle. According to James, the reflex arc extended from the external stimulation of the sense organs by the flame of a candle to a response from the internal organ of the brain, which in turn produced associations and beliefs ("habits"), specifically, the belief that placing one's hand in a flame will produce pain (Figure 1).

The theory of the reflex arc was tested in the European laboratories of Wilhelm Wundt and other experimental psychologists. While acknowledging the existence of external stimuli and responses, Wundt hypothesized the role of internal mental states including perception, awareness, attention, and cognition. All of these were thought to mediate external stimuli and responses. These internal mediating states could not be observed directly, but they could be inferred indirectly by measuring the elapsed time (in milliseconds) between

[10] Peirce's article is reproduced in L. Menand, ed., *Pragmatism: A Reader*. New York, NY: Vintage, 1997, pp. 7–48.

[11] In his William James Lectures at Harvard, Donald T. Campbell, the preeminent methodologist of public program evaluation as well as evolutionary epistemology, spoke of the 99:1 trust: doubt ratio that guides not only field experiments, but also change in science (Campbell and Stanley 1963: 6; Campbell 1988: 477).

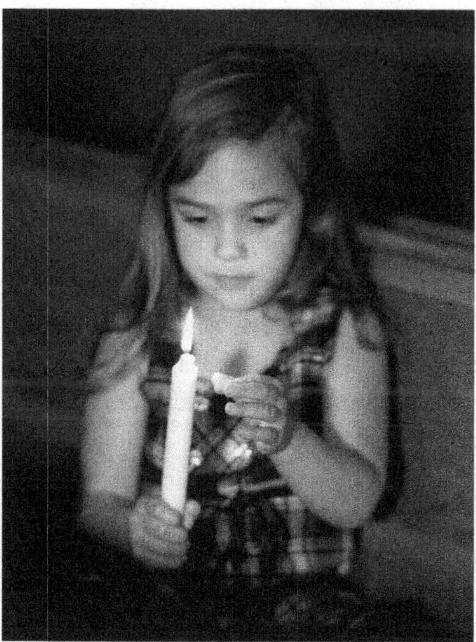

Figure 1 Candle experiment

the illumination of a light (the stimulus) and the act of pressing a lever (the response). The process elicited awareness, perception, or attention (the mediating mental states) that signaled that the light not only stimulated but mediated action when it was turned on.

The metaphor of the reflex arc, what Dewey eventually called a reflex *circle, cycle*, or *circuit*, carries great practical significance in representing core ideas of pragmatism. For Dewey and other pragmatists, the salient feature of the reflex arc was not that it began with a stimulus and ended in a response. Rather it was because the subjects introduced teleological reasoning into the movement of a stimulus and a response around the arc. Dewey's 1896 article exemplifies the strategy he followed in approaching most problems: seek to understand the ends, or values, that motivate individual and collective acts, ends, or values that are analogous to the stimuli (causes) and their responses (effects) in mechanistic processes.[12] "It is only when we regard the sequence of acts *as if* they were adapted to reach some *end* that it occurs to us to speak of one as stimulus and the other as response. Otherwise, we look at them as a *mere* series" (Dewey 1896: 370, n. 5, italics added).

[12] Dewey's instrumentalism, according to which concepts and beliefs are instruments of practical action, means that beliefs about manipulable stimuli qualify as instruments, which is a statement of his *experimentalism*.

This is a functionalist strategy, functional because base-values of wealth, enlightenment, power, well-being, skill, affection, respect, and rectitude (see Lasswell and Kaplan 1950) initiate functions in a decision process. This functionalist strategy is a major element of pragmatism and the policy sciences. For example, unless the end or value of a function is known, we cannot identify the presumed independent and dependent variables, or even whether we should treat training staff as a cost or a benefit in a logical framework (log frame) or program theory, both of which have a teleological component.

Dewey's organic theory of the reflex arc, cycle, or circuit appears later in Lasswell's theory of decisional functionalism (Lasswell 1956a, 1963). Stimulus and response are no longer parts of the mechanistic process described by Descartes, the "apperception" theory of Wundt, or later mechanistic misinterpretations of Lasswell's decision process. Stimulus and response are parts of an organic unity that begins, not with an external stimulus, but with the preference for one or more valued future outcomes. These preferred outcomes trigger a search for manipulable stimuli and resultant responses, or what we now call a "causal mechanism."

In the case of the candle, one future valued outcome is obtaining knowledge – or what Lasswell and McDougall (1943) refer to as *intelligence* – by learning about the flame through trial-and-error learning and experimentation. Experimentation, justified by Dewey's methodological doctrine of *experimentalism*, meant the abandonment of what Dewey called the "spectator theory of knowledge." For Dewey, experimentation was the primary way to learn and to know. The desire to obtain knowledge about the flame prompts the child to experiment by touching it, not by examining the flame from afar, as a spectator. The experiment elicits a painful response, followed by new (in this case painfully acquired) knowledge. Menand (1997: xxiii–xiv) describes this dynamic process:

> The results we get constitute a new piece of knowledge, which we carry over into our next encounter with our environment . . . Knowledge is not a mental copy of a reality external to us . . . it is an instrument or organ of successful action.[13]

Thus, knowledge is not founded on a correspondence of beliefs with nature (reality). Dewey the anti-dualist did not subscribe to the correspondence theory of truth that formed an essential part of Vienna Circle logical positivism decades

[13] See also W. Ascher and B. Hirschfelder-Ascher, *Revitalizing Political Psychology: The Legacy of Harold D. Lasswell*. New York, NY: Lawrence Erlbaum, 2004. The Aschers also point out the connection between postpositivism and fallibilism: "[P]ragmatism already exhibited the insights shared with postpositivism that are crucial for justifying the status of psychodynamic functional theory: the recognition that ultimate certainty is unattainable" (p. 7).

later (Ascher and Hirschfelder-Ascher 2004: 7–8). Dewey's epistemology of instrumentalism saw the learner as an active participant in changing experiences, "a living organism with her own history, needs, desires, and ... interests"(Hickman 2009: 8). Similarly, the anti-dualist, although she abandons dualist correspondence theory, is not a relativist, but rather a proponent of *objective relativism*. Here, "truth" is objectively corroborated, relative to the presumptively known object, but it cannot be defined entirely in terms of the social circumstances or subjective states of the knower (Kaplan 1964: 392–393). The principle of objective relativism expresses the unity of subject and object, theory and practice, contemplation and action.

Given its complexity, Dewey's reflex arc deserves his own label, the *reflex circuit*. The complex relations that define a circuit provide a suitably intricate framework for investigating policy adaptation and change by focusing on values that, singly and in their overall configuration, guide the behaviors of individuals and groups that for pragmatists are organic wholes – not thoughtless mechanisms incapable of self-referential action. Above all, the reflex circuit helps frame the seven functions of the decision process (Lasswell 1956a) that, arguably, are among the most important of Lasswell's contributions to the policy sciences. Although a detailed examination of Lasswell's decisional functions awaits later discussion, Lasswell's framework of the decision process has four essential properties that originate in pragmatism and the reflex circuit.

Policy Change Is Adaptive. Outcomes of each function of the decision process constitute the achievement of values – for example, wealth, well-being, skill, and respect – that are carried over into the next decisional function. Intelligence is carried over to prescription and appraisal. Base-values are not fixed. They change because of adaptation to new functional demands.[14] Bromley (2006: 24) and other economists have stressed that, if ends are given or fixed, as in utility maximization, "all that remains is for the individual to compute the most efficacious means to achieve those ends ... as long as the individual could not 'rationally' have done other than what the calculations revealed to be the rational choice, the agent did not exercise choice." Indeed, this kind of pseudo-choice preempts the achievement of values and their adaptation.

Policy Change May Be Represented As a Circuit. Decisional functions are not linear. Although Lasswell (1956a: 97) proposes that changes are cyclical, changes are sufficiently complex that the term *circuit* better fits his statement

[14] Ascher and Hirschfelder-Ascher emphasize that Deweyan functionalism must be distinguished from the later structural functional theory of Talcott Parsons (Parsons 1949).

that "every agency of government is involved in varying degree with every function; and ... all component parts of ... society are expected to express themselves at least through the electorate" (Lasswell 1956a: 95). Hence, the process is one that may be characterized as cycles within cycles – or wheels within wheels – and not the simple cyclical processes described in the comprehensive literature review by Jann and Wegrich (2007). Decisional functions are, rather, like a complex circuit. Linearity or simple cyclicality are not properties of change in Dewey's reflex arc or in Lasswell's seven functions of the decision process.

The Relation between Base-Values and Decisional Functions Is Abductive. Adaptation and change in decisional functions follow the choice of values, which are contextual "ends in view," rather than lexical fixed ends that fail to reflect the teleological reason of individuals with the capacity to make genuine choices among alternative values. Base-values (Lasswell and Kaplan 1950) are abductive because they "go back to" decisional functions, functions that are instruments for achieving those values. The process of abduction is not deductive, as in rational choice theory, or inductive, as in survey experiments or ethnography, because in policy contexts, as in everyday life, we regularly deal with indeterminate situations, anomalies, or surprises that Dewey and others have called "problem situations" (Ackoff 1974a: 237–239; Rein and White 1977: 262).

Decisional Functions Are Complex. The complexity of decisional functions is a consequence of change and adaptation within and across functions, and of the fact that policies are not single decisions, but configurations of decisions. Different policies perform more than one function. Chester Barnard (1938), who was a key influence on Lasswell and, notably, students at Chicago like Herbert Simon (see Easton 1950), captured the complexity of decisions when he described the decision to relocate a telephone pole from one side of the street to another.[15] Barnard, a successful CEO and classic contributor to public and business administration, suggested that moving the telephone pole

> involves perhaps 10,000 decisions of 100 men located at 15 points, requiring successive analyses of several environments, including social, moral, legal, economic, and physical facts of the environment, and requiring 9,000 redefinitions and refinements of purpose. [However,] not more than half-a-dozen decisions will be recalled or deemed worthy of mention ... The others will be "taken for granted." (Barnard 1938: 198)

[15] I am indebted to the late Carol H. Weiss for directing my attention to this example from Barnard.

2 The Chicago School of Pragmatism

The policy sciences grew out of Lasswell's studies, teaching, and research at the University of Chicago, where he earned a BA in philosophy and economics in 1922. In 1924, he and Willard E. Atkins coauthored a book on labor economics titled *Labor Attitudes and Problems* (Atkins and Lasswell 1924). An early example of a policy orientation, the book investigated the work, life, and leisure of coal miners and steel workers, focusing on the risks faced by labor: machinery and industrial accidents, chronic illness, destitution in old age, and unemployment. When Lasswell began graduate studies in political science, the department was the smallest in the social sciences, with four faculty including Charles Merriam. Harry Pratt Judson, who specialized in comparative constitutional law, headed it. Nevertheless, by 1926, Lasswell completed a PhD under the direction of his mentor, Charles E. Merriam, who is generally regarded as one of the main founders of the behavioral (scientific) movement in political science.

2.1 Chicago Antecedents

One antecedent of the policy sciences was *Methods in the Social Sciences* (1931), a book of cases edited by Stuart Rice and organized by Harold Lasswell. The volume grew out of Merriam's efforts, as president of the Social Science Research Council, to integrate the social sciences. From roughly 1925 to 1938, graduate students and faculty in philosophy, political science, sociology, and psychology departments were united, with few exceptions, by a common commitment to Dewey's pragmatism. Dewey came to call his variant of pragmatism *instrumentalism* (or pragmatist instrumentalism) to distinguish his version of pragmatism from that of Peirce. Dewey also differed because he was committed to a functionalist theory of society and human behavior (Bulmer 1984: 29–30; Ascher and Hirschfelder-Ascher 2004). Significantly, Lasswell would later define the policy sciences as the creation of "knowledge *of* and *in* the decision processes of the public and civic order" (Lasswell 1971b: 1). This definition, which mirrors Dewey's instrumentalism, reflects Lasswell's pragmatist orientation toward the social sciences, just as his functionalist perspectives were reflected in his work on functions of the decision process (Lasswell 1956a). Although the social sciences were not at that time called *policy sciences*, they were nevertheless embedded in what Lasswell called the Chicago prototype of a "cross-disciplinary manifold" (Lasswell 1971b: 416–428). In the context of 1930s Chicago, a cross-disciplinary manifold was an intellectual space that houses social science disciplines. Numerous openings allow different disciplines and subdisciplines to enter and exit. In Lasswell's terms, the "manifold" permitted disciplines to affect each other, with cross-cutting ties between and within the disciplines.

> Because the Chicago philosophy reflected an awareness of the interconnections among the advances being made in biology, psychology, and sociology, it was able to provide a method and a perspective for an array of disciplines. And so it was that Chicago was a school . . . it was a school with a philosophy full of its progeny. The progeny were as much products of the susceptibility of the new university to untraditional approaches to academic matters as they were of the fecundity of the philosophy. The institutional atmosphere of new beginnings made for an audacity and an experimental spirit in certain areas that could not be expected in more established universities or in more traditional disciplines. Psychology, education, religion, sociology, economics, and political science . . . were already in ferment, and at Chicago the Philosophy Department was developing ideas in a form readily relevant to problems in those fields. (Rucker 1969: vii)

Chicago's cross-disciplinary experiment was moribund by 1938. This did not happen naturally, because of demographic or financial changes external to the university, or because of generational change and retirements from within. It was rather that Chicago president Robert Maynard Hutchins took recruitment actions that, coincident with generational change, negatively affected the departments of philosophy and political science (Bulmer 1984: 202). As Rucker (1969: 26) writes:

> [T]he Chicago School came to a definite end in 1931. It seems typical of the University of Chicago that the close of that important era did not take place with the quiet retirement of the remaining patriarchs of the department . . . but instead was marked by a flurry of resignations amidst considerable uproar, both in the university and the city. A good pragmatist is never merely a theoretician of action.

By 1938, Hutchins, who denied Harold Lasswell and Charles E. Gosnell promotion to full professor, had decimated the political science department. Lasswell departed for Yale, where previously, in 1932, he had provided advice on the first policy sciences course offered for lawyers. Gosnell, a respected political scientist, left Chicago in 1942.

2.2 Dewey's Influence

From 1894 to 1904, Dewey headed the joint philosophy and psychology department at Chicago. While appointed primarily as a philosopher, Dewey had already published a textbook, *Psychology*, in 1887. Dewey accepted the appointment at Chicago after completing his doctorate at Johns Hopkins University and spending some ten years at the University of Michigan.

At Hopkins, Dewey studied with Charles Sanders Peirce, who with William James was the most influential of the founding philosophical pragmatists (Menand 2001: 337–375). At Chicago, Dewey's pragmatism affected all the social sciences, as did the pragmatism of philosopher and social psychologist George Herbert Mead, whom Dewey had brought from Michigan. In 1904, Dewey departed for Columbia University with his wife, Alice, who had been denied promotion as head of the Chicago Laboratory School, which Dewey had helped to establish.

Although Dewey's tenure at Chicago was cut short after he left for Columbia in 1904, his influence endured for the next generation, in part because he had brought a robust contingent of pragmatists from Johns Hopkins and from the University of Michigan. The contingent of pragmatists included philosophers and social scientists who worked in different areas: Addison W. Moore and Edward S. Ames in philosophy, William I. Thomas and Robert Park in sociology, George Herbert Mead in philosophy, sociology, and social psychology, and institutional economists Frank Knight and Thorstein Veblen. Robert Park, who developed and conducted systematic surveys of the immigrant population in Chicago, had studied with William James. Park celebrated pragmatism, as manifested in surveys of the Chicago population in which the results were fed back for problem-solving purposes to individuals and groups. Park conducted and organized policy-relevant research in the city of Chicago. Park was one of Lasswell's more influential mentors (Coughlan 1973: ch. 9; Carey 1975: ch. 6).

Bulmer (1984: 29) succinctly captures the influence of pragmatism on the social sciences at Chicago: "[T]he Chicago school of pragmatist philosophy extended over a generation of Chicago social science, setting the tone and providing a general orientation to scientific inquiry." In late 1903, William James paid tribute to Dewey's achievements:

> Chicago University has during the past six months given birth to the fruits of ten years of gestation under John Dewey. The result is wonderful – a *real school* and *real thought* . . . Here [at Harvard] we have thought, but no school. At Yale a school but no thought. Chicago has both. (quoted by Bulmer 1984: 28, italics original)

2.3 The Cross-Disciplinary Manifold

Between 1915 and 1938, philosophy, sociology, and other social sciences flourished, markedly influencing the development of the social sciences in the United States and Western Europe. Lasswell termed the pragmatist institutional network that shaped this achievement the "cross-disciplinary manifold" (Lasswell 1971a). The "manifold" may be visualized as a set of institutional properties including the dates of interaction among Lasswell's teachers, mentors, and colleagues, the focus of their disciplines and their research products, and their status as what Deutsch, Platt, and Senghaas (1970: 373–420) call advances in the social sciences. The rough map of judgments about advancements in theory, methodology, substantive findings, and practical applications (Table 1) is based on Deutsch, Markovits, and Platt, *Advances in the Social Sciences, 1900–1980* (1986).[16]

2.4 Focus on Public Policy

Although the social sciences and philosophy earned an unjustified reputation for unbridled empiricism, Bulmer (1984: ch. 12) and others Carey (1975: ch. 6) provide evidence of a close relationship between pragmatist philosophers and psychologists, sociologists, and political scientists. In the early period, Dewey was the preponderant influence, while George Herbert Mead, whom Dewey originally brought from Michigan, had the greater impact in the 1920s. The leader of the sociologists, Robert E. Park, was a self-conscious pragmatist who developed survey, case study, ethnographic, and life-history methods while studying the working class of Chicago. Park had a significant influence on Lasswell (Bulmer 1984: 125–126), who attended his seminars on research methods and worked as his research assistant. Park as well as the other leading sociologist, Ernest W. Burgess, would today be seen as champions of the application of mixed or multiple methods in research on urban problems.

The approach to all the social sciences was multidisciplinary and applied. In the area of public policy, William S. Ogburn, the quantitative sociologist, worked on President Hoover's Commission on Recent Social Trends, as did Merriam, Gosnell, and other political scientists. Lasswell and Leonard B. White were carrying out pioneering studies in political science, while psychologist L. L. Thurstone was designing methods of attitude measurement that contributed to economic research on expected utility measurement in experimental economics (Kagel and Roth 1995: 5–6). Economist Henry Schultz was laying the foundations of econometrics. Jacob Viner and Frank Knight were developing institutional economics. While there was a general expectation that social

[16] The Deutsch et al. list of advances in the social sciences, like the list of awardees of the Sverige Riksbank Prize in Economic Sciences (awarded in memory of Alfred Nobel), is not without disagreement as to the validity of these appraisals. Nevertheless, the Deutsch et al. advances, because very few are in "economic sciences," do not qualify for the Swedish National Bank award, although they are its functional equivalent. The noneconomic advances, many of which are multidisciplinary, outnumber those of their economic counterparts at Chicago and elsewhere.

Table 1 Cross-Disciplinary Manifold, 1915–1955

Member	Discipline	Period of Involvement	Philosophical Influence	Professional Influence	Type of Advance
John Dewey	Philosophy Psychology Education	1894–1904	Pragmatism	James Peirce Mead Addams	Theory Practice
George H. Mead	Philosophy Psychology Sociology	1894–1931	Pragmatism	Dewey Addams	Theory Findings Practice
Charles Merriam	Political Science Sociology	1900–1940	Logical Empiricism	Dewey	Theory Methods Findings Practice
Robert Park	Sociology Journalism	1914–1933	Pragmatism	James Dewey	Theory Methods Findings Practice
W. I. Thomas	Psychology	1895–1920	Pragmatism	Dewey	Theory Methods Findings
H. Simon	Political Science Economics	1933–1943	Logical Empiricism Pragmatism	Barnard Park Merriam	Theory Methods Findings

F. Knight	Institutional Economics	1929–1955	Pragmatism	Dewey Thurstone	Theory Methods Findings
J. H. Tufts	Philosophy Psychology	1892–1930	Pragmatism	James Dewey	Theory Methods Findings
J. R. Angell	Philosophy Psychology	1895–1921	Pragmatism	James Dewey	Theory Methods Findings
T. Veblen	Institutional Economics	1892–1909	Pragmatism	Peirce Dewey	Theory Methods Findings

science research would contribute solutions to social problems, there was also a focus on democracy and social betterment. This same normative and democratic orientation later appeared in virtually all the work of Lasswell and McDougal in the policy sciences.

Jane Addams and the Hull House Papers are also exemplary of the policy-oriented, reformist, democratic orientation of philosophy and the social sciences in Chicago. The pragmatism of Dewey, James, and Peirce appealed to Addams, and she and Dewey were colleagues, friends, and collaborators. Dewey was a frequent visitor to Hull House before and after leaving Chicago for Columbia. Addams was also close with George Herbert Mead, the pragmatist social psychologist and creator of symbolic interactionism; their influence was mutual. Addams received the Nobel Prize in 1936, and she is credited with founding the American Civil Liberties Union (ACLU). Students at Chicago read Addams's books and, while she would not accept a regular appointment, Addams taught as an adjunct professor.

2.5 Financial and Research Infrastructure

The financial and research infrastructure, including the erection of new buildings, was characteristic of the cross-disciplinary manifold and the Chicago model (Goodspeed 1916; Storr 1966; see Boyer 2015). The search for outside financial support, for example, from the Carnegie Corporation and the Spelman Rockefeller Memorial Fund, was successful. The Social Science Research Building, which was designed to house the Local Community Research Committee – an interdisciplinary and policy-oriented institution – included a large statistical archive and what then was the most advanced equipment for carrying out statistical analyses (Bulmer 1984: 195–197).

A virtually unique feature of the Social Science Research Building, at least in the late 1920s, was its deliberate departure from the disciplinary design of the vast majority of social science buildings, which is that of a separate floor, wing, or entire building to house separate disciplines. Instead, the Social Science Research Building mixed faculty from different disciplines, much like a contemporary matrix organization. Ogburn, the eminent quantitative sociologist, was adjacent to Harold Gosnell, the political scientist who conducted urban surveys; psychologist L. L. Thurstone and the labs for economic experiments were adjacent to Lasswell; Schultz, the economist, was next to Herbert Blumer, the qualitative sociologist.

The image of Chicago in these early years is like a cross-disciplinary manifold encased in brick and mortar. Given these material-cum-intellectual innovations, it is tempting to conclude that Chicago's deliberate interdisciplinarity reflects a philosophically pragmatist design to break down the dualism of disciplines, not by ignoring their disciplinary advantages for developing theory and research, but concurrently by seeking *unity*. As Menand (2001: 324) tells us, unity is the fighting word of pragmatism.

2.6 The Decline of the Cross-Disciplinary Manifold

Given the efficacy and robustness of multidisciplinary, policy-oriented social science at Chicago after 1915, the policy sciences, formally proposed between 1932 and 1951 at Yale (McDougal and Lasswell 1943; Lerner and Lasswell 1951), may be regarded as a "second-best" solution to the recovery of the cross-disciplinary manifold at Chicago. The Chicago model (Lasswell 1971a) represented an institutional matrix that was already policy-oriented, multidisciplinary, and contextual, the three characteristics that Lasswell enunciated as defining characteristics of the policy sciences in 1951.

The Chicago School, apart from close connections with the policy sciences, also represented the rise of policy-oriented empirical research in a new university setting. A distinctive advantage of Chicago was its relatively recent establishment (1898), which provided the university with many fewer traditions and constraints, particularly requirements to teach the classics and general philosophy, subjects in which Chicago did not specialize until the advent of Hutchins's "great books" program. It was comparatively difficult to innovate at old schools such as Harvard, Princeton, and Yale. As Bulmer (1984: ch. 12) argues, many of the most important conditions for intellectual and institutional creativity were at Chicago.

Between 1915 and 1938, Chicago dominated the policy-oriented social sciences in the United States. The "schools" that made up the university – philosophy, psychology, sociology, political science – and the Chicago School of Pragmatism, the "mega-school" that owed its existence to Dewey, enjoyed freedom that the older Ivy League universities did not have until the mid-twentieth century. The Chicago schools led a movement away from general social and political theory, political philosophy, and history, "toward the first-hand empirical investigation of society by means of personal documents, observations, and interviewing, conducted within an implicit general theoretical framework"(Bulmer 1984: xiii). The community of scholars and cross-fertile institutions of Chicago appear to be rare in the history of the social sciences. The survey of advances in the social sciences between 1900 and 1980 by Deutsch and colleagues (1986) profiles fifty major advances in the social sciences, some 36 percent of which occurred at Chicago between 1910 and

1938.[17] Of the total, five were Lasswell's advances in areas of psychology, communications theory, content analysis, propaganda, and the policy sciences.

By 1938, political science and philosophy were moribund (Almond 2004), a condition created by President Hutchins. Under Hutchins, Lasswell and other social scientists got a reputation for conducting "vulgar empiricist research," which was among the reasons that Lasswell and Gosnell were denied promotion to the rank of full professor. Mortimer Adler, reflecting his and Hutchins's preference for philosophical abstraction and normative ethics, replaced the head of philosophy. A journalist from *Fortune* contrasted Hutchins's position with that of Dewey:

> Even those who are willing to admit Hutchins's preoccupation with values, with the oughts of life, are unwilling to grant the final authority to the Aristotelian tradition to define values. They [Dewey and others] insist that no values can be fixed, and [argue] that a valid modern philosophy need not reckon with ideas as they are expressed in the books of ancient and mediaeval times. (Adler 1977: 184)

The unity of theory and practice was realized by means of a *configural* approach that self-consciously combined the contemplative and the practical, rather than keeping them apart in a dualistic relation. Much of this unity was lost with the decline of the political science and philosophy departments. Gabriel Almond, an eminent contributor to the fields of political culture and comparative political participation, and one of Lasswell's students at Chicago, also reports that the final blow to political science came from Hutchins (Almond 2004). Part of what was lost was what later became the four legs of the policy sciences: problem-oriented inquiry, contextual analysis, multiple qualitative and quantitative methods, and a normative commitment to human dignity and allied social values.

3 Functions of the Decision Process

The *decision* is one of the most important concepts in Lasswell's theory of the policy sciences. In turn, the policy sciences provide the framework for the decision process, which is its virtual heart. Lasswell and Kaplan, as early as 1950, defined the decision as "a projected course of action designed to bring about goal values and practices through the exercise of power" (Lasswell and Kaplan 1950: 71). The decision process was limited to decision makers who actually formulate, communicate, and apply policies – those we now call "stakeholders" – who affect and are affected

[17] I have omitted from the Deutsch et al. list mathematics and political organizing (e.g., Lenin, Mao-Tse Tung, Mahatma Gandhi).

by a particular decision, and not by an abstract unitary actor such as a firm or a collective (see Lasswell and Kaplan 1950: 74–75).

3.1 The Concept of Decision

David Easton, who joined the University of Chicago after Lasswell's departure, reports that Lasswell was sufficiently impressed by the concept of decision to adopt it from Chester Barnard, via one of his students, Herbert A. Simon, and to further develop it for the study of policy (Easton 1950: 472).[18] However, Lasswell, McDougal, and others seem to have discovered the concept of decision as early as the 1930s, perhaps from unnamed German sources, but more likely from the legal realists at Yale, Myres McDougal and Thurman Arnold, who taught the 1932 seminar on the policy sciences. The concept of the decision had been vital to the realist tradition of jurisprudence, at least from the time of Oliver Wendell Holmes, a colleague of William James and other pragmatists. Holmes's opposition to legal formalism would later mark him as a key influence in the development of legal realism (Menand 2001: 438–439). The concept of the decision, fundamental to realism, eventually influenced Herbert Simon's dissertation, which was later published as *Administrative Behavior* (Simon 1947), a classic on administrative decision-making. As noted earlier, Simon, one of Lasswell's students at Chicago, adopted the concept of decision from Chester Barnard, the preeminent administrative theorist and author of another classic, *The Functions of the Executive* (Barnard 1938).

Easton (1950: 247) describes Lasswell's adoption of the concept:

> With the emergence of the decision-making approach there opens up a new path for a rigorous search after verifiable generalizations about political behavior. In the first place, an operational definition of power can now be approached. Power, Lasswell states, is an influential decision, that is, a decision which involves severe sanctions or deprivations.

In a footnote, Easton (1950: 247 n) directs readers to "an intensive analysis of the use of the decisional approach, applied in this case to the area of public administration, in the extremely suggestive work of Herbert Alexander Simon, *Administrative Behavior* (New York: Macmillan Company, 1947)." Lasswell's own decisional approach, in contrast to that of Simon, is a form of *functional*

[18] Analyses of co-citations of papers written by Lasswell, Barnard, Simon, Lindblom, and Wildavsky show that the link between Lasswell and Barnard is stronger than links with Lindblom, Simon, and Wildavsky (Lindblom's student). See Corbacıoğlu (2008). It is instructive to consider the similarity in perspectives of Lindblom and Cohen (1979) and Hayek (1945) on the use of knowledge in society. By contrast, Barnard, as well as Dewey (see Lasswell 1956b), influenced Lasswell's perspectives.

decision theory that may be traced to Dewey's reflex arc. The basic unit of analysis is the class of decisions called functions. The rationale for grouping decisions under functions was that "when we are dealing with activities that display the infinite variations in institutional practices to be found in government, it is important not to lose sight of the forest by becoming preoccupied with naming the trees … it is not a question of arriving at a permanent classification … classifications are serviceable when they are tentative and undogmatic" (1956a: 93).

3.2 The Decision Process

During his years at Yale, Lasswell wrote one of his most important contributions to the study of the policy-making process, *The Decision Process: Seven Categories of Functional Analysis* (Lasswell 1956a). This short monograph, which was one of many products of his collaboration with McDougal, was a mere twenty-three pages in length. Nevertheless, it contains a virtually complete account of Lasswell's perspectives of the decision process. For this reason, among others, the monograph deserves more attention than it has received among policy scholars and mainstream political scientists, who have often learned about Lasswell's ideas by reading secondary sources such as Jones (1977) and Anderson (2011).

The 1956 monograph presents policy making as a series of functionally organized decisions, or purposive acts, designed to achieve the goal of human dignity and associated "base-values." Earlier, with Abraham Kaplan, the pragmatist philosopher of science and methodologist, Lasswell had identified a virtually exhaustive range of eight base-values: power, wealth, enlightenment, well-being, skill, affection, respect, and rectitude. These base-values, which are realized through the decision process, have the form of a practical inference (or practical syllogism), which figures prominently in the (Aristotelian) tradition of teleological reasoning and final cause.[19] Georg von Wright (1971:2-3)contrasts this tradition with the (Galilean) tradition of mechanistic causality. The basic form of the practical inference is:

Decision maker, *d*, intends to bring about the goal, *g*, of human dignity.
Decision maker, *d*, considers that she cannot bring about the goal, *g*, of human dignity unless she does act, *a*.
Therefore, *d* acts to achieve *a*.

[19] Base-values are general categories of values, each of which has derived variants, for example, savings, investment, and property ownership are variants of wealth.

3.3 Decisional Functionalism

Easton (1950) called Lasswell's decision process *decisional functionalism*, one important characteristic of which is that it is a form of practical inference. Lasswell's decision process is a set of seven decisional functions carried out by governments. The seven decisional functions, with illustrative outcomes, are presented in what follows. The eight base-values identified by Lasswell and Kaplan (1950) are expected effects of the decision process.[20]

As Menand (2001: 324) tells us, "[u]nity is the fighting word of functionalism." In this context, functionalism is what unifies decisions and values. This means that theory and practice, contemplation and action, valuation and decision, are of one part; they are not dualistic entities. This anti-dualistic perspective is one of the principal epistemological characteristics of pragmatism.

The *decision* is the central underlying concept in Lasswell's decision process. Chester Barnard's concept of decision, as presented in *The Functions of the Executive* (1938), was pivotal in reconceptualizing processes of policy making. Barnard, as noted earlier, was a major influence on Simon's dissertation at Chicago (Barnard wrote the preface) and Simon's subsequent major contribution to public administration, *Administrative Behavior: A Study of Decision Making Processes in Administrative Organizations* (Simon 1947). In turn, Simon's dissertation, like Lasswell's work on the decision process, became a classic in public administration.

3.4 The Maximization Postulate

A factor that explains changes of decision functions, and that serves to stimulate hypotheses, is what Lasswell (1956a:10) called the "maximization postulate." The postulate states that:

> [P]eople do what they do in the hope of being better off than if they did otherwise. To be better off is assessed in terms of the values, the preferred events, of the persons concerned. In general, the postulate holds that any change in function comes about because the change is expected to maximize the value position of those who make it. The task of research is to explore hypotheses suggested by this postulate.[21]

[20] Lasswell states that values are effects of outcomes. The distinction between outcomes and effects is awkward, as originally stated by Lasswell. Another way to state the distinction is to use the terms *proximal* and *intermediate outcomes*, reserving the term *distal outcome* for impact. This is consistent with the language and logic of program theory in evaluation research.

[21] Lasswell later stated the maximization postulate somewhat differently: "[L]iving forms are predisposed to complete acts in ways that are perceived to leave the actor better off than if he

The maximization postulate has been viewed, erroneously, as an expression of expected economic utility. A more accurate interpretation is what Lasswell (1956b: 12) called "maximization analysis," a general method for explaining subjectively meaningful acts (Brunner 1991: 77–78; see also Torgerson 1985 and Brown 2002). The maximization postulate may also be seen as a statement about the operation of interpretive understanding (*Verstehen*) in motivating individual acts (Kaplan 1964: 142–143). Interpretive understanding may be extended to embrace decisions among two or more persons who are motivated by different goals and values, an inconsistency that calls for a process of values clarification (Lasswell and McDougal 1992: 229–267). Values clarification involves the examination of alternative decisions from the standpoint of realist, positivist, historical, sociological, and other perspectives.

For Lasswell and others, the adoption of functional decision theory shifted the focus toward authoritative decisions and away from elites as the source of power. Authoritative decisions capture segments of a community that may be identified as elite, but without reifying the concept of "elite" without first investigating the decision makers who compose it. "An authoritative decision is part of a process, or of a context of interaction, that has achieved a high degree of stability" (McDougal, Lasswell, and Reisman 1967: 298). Decisions, and not the rules or general principles of Fayol (1916) and Gulick and Urwick (1937), became the focus.

3.5 Barnard's Decision Complex

The importance of the concept of decision and the decision process, as distinguished from older elitist approaches to decision-making, can be readily appreciated by considering Barnard's account of a manager faced with the decision to move a telephone pole from one side of the street to the other. We might focus on statutory rules to determine whether the policy (moving the telephone pole) is lawful or unlawful. Alternatively, we might focus on analytical rules such as the rule that moving the pole must have net benefits greater than zero, or a cost-benefit ratio greater than unity. On the other hand, using management principles, we might ask engineers to move the pole, based on the principle of delegation within a hierarchical chain of command.

However, Barnard's account yields a very different conclusion:

had completed them differently. The postulate draws attention to the actor's own perception of the alternative act completions open to him in a given situation" (Lasswell 197b: 16).

> It can, I think, be approximately demonstrated that carrying out that order involves perhaps 10,000 decisions of 100 men located at 15 points, requiring successive analyses of several environments, including social, moral, legal, economic, and physical facts of the environment, and requiring 9,000 redefinitions and refinements of purpose. If inquiry be made of those responsible, probably not more than half-a-dozen decisions will be recalled or deemed worthy of mention ... The others will be "taken for granted," all of a part of the business of knowing one's business. (Barnard 1938: 198)

An image of simple linearity or of mono-cyclicality is plainly inconsistent with Lasswell and McDougal's representation of the decision process. To be sure, Lasswell and McDougal use the term *sequential decision process*, which suggests that preceding decisional functions come before succeeding ones – for example, prescriptive decisions must occur before decisions to apply them – but Lasswell and McDougal also represent decisional functions as categories of complex decisions. For example, in discussing the decisions that make up the intelligence function, McDougal, Lasswell, and Reisman (1972: 366–367) argue that the need for intelligence permeates every decisional function, from decisions about promotion and prescription to decisions about application, termination, and appraisal. Dewey, it must be emphasized, saw what he called the "general method of intelligence" as a form of practical reasoning directed toward some value or "end in view." An end in view is a naturally experienced end that arises in a specific context, rather than an abstract or formal end or purpose.

3.6 The Intelligence Function

As we have seen, decisions within the intelligence function involve the acquisition of information required to exercise five intellectual tasks: goal clarification, trend description, analysis of conditions influencing trend, projection of future developments, and invention, evaluation, and selection of alternatives (Lasswell 1971: 39). The intelligence function involves three activities: information gathering, processing, and dissemination. The effectiveness of these activities depends upon the efficacy of coding, assembling, storing, decoding, retrieving, and interpreting information (McDougal et al. 1972: 368). Moreover, the intelligence function is constituted by decisions performed both technically and in relation to the social process. The social process is composed of agencies, organizations, groups, and individuals who, operating with different perspectives, make contextually specific decisions using different strategies to achieve their values.

This description of the intelligence function, when considered alongside Barnard's case of the telephone pole, suggests that thousands of decisions must be performed in order to collect, process, and disseminate information. While Jenkins-Smith and Sabatier (1993) believe that Lasswell's perspective of the decision process is inherently incapable of reflecting the complexity of intergovernmental relations, the decision process described by McDougal and Lasswell by no means precludes decisional functions with complex patterns of decision that are linear and nonlinear, cyclical and multi-cyclical, arborescent (branch-and-tree) and assembly (tree-and-branch), single and parallel processing, or a combination of these patterns (see Dunn 1988; Brunner 1997).

Thus, Lasswell's decision process is more complex than the simple sequential model posited by critics. Falk and colleagues (1998: 729–730) point to the scope and complexity of the Lasswell-McDougal model. In the 1940s, when Yale was a center of legal realism, there was an effort to challenge legal positivism by recognizing that law is no more than the decisions of human beings. The legal realists successfully demonstrated that rules alone could not explain why past decisions had been made or how future decisions were likely to be made.

3.7 Contextuality, Methodological Diversity, and the Policy Orientation

As we have seen, a focus on the actions involved in making a decision led Lasswell (1956a) to develop a contingent analysis of decision-making that was broken down into the functions of intelligence, promotion, prescription, invocation, application, appraisal, and termination. Lasswell and McDougal (1943) had earlier aspired to teach future scholars and lawyers, who in the 1940s and 1950s, were the counterparts of contemporary high-level policy analysts and advisors. Lasswell and McDougal believed that the policy sciences must be contextual, that is, take into account features of the social process. The policy sciences must also be problem-oriented and, given the large number of contextual variations that must be investigated, they must employ multiple methods. Although it was not clear to members of the New Haven School whether the joint requirement of contextuality and effective practical application could be satisfied, McDougal and Lasswell nevertheless insisted that we attend to social and power processes, as had sociologically oriented students of jurisprudence. Nevertheless, in addition to its explicit normative orientation, the conceptual framework of the policy sciences has retained three components. "The first is *contextuality*: decisions are part of a larger social process. The second is *problem orientation*: policy scientists are at home with the intellectual activities involved in clarifying goals, trends, conditions, projections, and alternatives. The third is [methodological] *diversity*: The methods employed are not limited to a narrow range" (Lasswell 1971b: 4. Italics original).

3.8 The Seven Decisional Functions

In his 1956 monograph on functions of the decision process, Lasswell (1956a: 1–2) sought to replace overly simple concepts of legislative, executive, and judicial functions with a wider and more realistic array of seven functions, each of which answered a specific question:

Intelligence. How is the information that comes to the attention of decision makers gathered and processed? Outcomes of the intelligence function include gathering, processing, and disseminating information for the use of participants in the decision process, for example regulatory agencies and judicial bodies. Values of enlightenment, wealth, and skill are among the possible effects of gathering, processing, and disseminating information.

Promotion. How are recommendations made and promoted among stakeholders? Outcomes of the promotion function include agitation and propaganda for the use of leaders, political parties, and interest groups. Values of power and skill are among the possible effects of agitation and propaganda.

Prescription. How are general rules (e.g., legislative acts) prescribed? Outcomes of the prescriptive function include the routinization and institutionalization of enforceable norms by executives and legislators. Values of power, respect, and skill are among the possible effects of executive orders, legislative acts, and other enforceable norms.

Invocation. How are general rules provisionally invoked in reference to conduct? Outcomes of the invocation function include enforced conformity to prescriptions among staff of line agencies. The possible effects of enforced conformity are power, wealth, and rectitude.

Application. How are general rules applied? Outcomes of the application function include written documentation by appellate court judges of conditions under which prescriptions must be applied. Values of skill, respect, and rectitude are possible effects of cases written by appellate court judges.

Appraisal. How is the operation of prescriptions to be appraised? Outcomes of the appraisal function include the assignment of legal or administrative responsibility for the assessment of policy objectives. Values of wealth, power, and enlightenment are possible effects of the assessment of objectives by means of investigative commissions, inspectors general, and research offices of legislatures.

Termination. Outcomes of the termination function include the adjudication of claims of parties affected by the cancellation of prescriptions. Values of power and well-being are among the possible effects of adjudicating cases before small claims courts.[22]

Lasswell later revised the seven original decisional functions in *A Pre-View of Policy Sciences* (1971b). This was his last major work on the policy sciences before his death in 1978. At first glance, the book appears to present a typical theory of sequential decision-making. Sequential theories typically begin with a policy problem, followed by a sequence of activities directed toward its solution, for example, formulation, adoption, implementation, evaluation, adaptation, and termination (e.g., Jones 1977 and Anderson 2011).[23] However, Lasswell's decisions are contingent, with some decisions necessarily preceding later decisions – for example, recommendation must logically precede prescription.

3.9 Decisional Functions and Practical Reasoning

Lasswell's decisions are also called functions, not stages, a difference of pivotal theoretical and practical importance. In this context, Lasswell follows Dewey (1922: 224–225) in viewing a function as a purposeful (or teleological) act, not simply as a set of decisions. Functions, as observed earlier, may be traced to a tradition of practical reasoning associated with Aristotle and developed by later interpretivist theorists including Heidegger, Weber, and Gadamer. Georg Henrik von Wright's treatise on theories of explanation and understanding (1971) shows that acts of practical reasoning are decisions about future states of affairs involving the achievement of some purpose. Achieving a purpose is a consequence of making decisions, or choices, about future states of affairs, rather than applying rules or principles to existing data. Decision-making, write McDougal and colleagues (1967: 254), "is not a body of rules, but . . . a process of making authoritative decisions about the production and distribution of values in the community . . . Rules alone could not explain why past decisions had been made or how future decisions were likely to be made."

Although the Lasswell model is grounded in some of the same concerns with the complexity of decision-making that led Simon toward the concept

[22] In other writings, Lasswell (1971b) places the appraisal function after termination, giving rise to criticism that it is illogical that Lasswell placed termination before appraisal.

[23] Jones, following Lasswell and Dewey, recognizes functions and not simply staged activities.

of "bounded rationality," Lasswell's decision process bears almost no resemblance to the partisan mutual adjustment-disjointed incrementalism model of Lindblom (1965) and Braybrooke and Lindblom (1963). The latter model is partly based on the fundamentally different theoretical foundation supplied by Friedrich Hayek and other Austrian economists (Adelstein 1992; see also Lindblom 1991). Here, complex social and economic systems are seen as largely (but not entirely) self-regulating, similar to a free market, protected by laws governing property rights, and resistant to the kinds of research interventions promoted by Lasswell and other policy scientists.

In this context, Corbacıoğlu (2008) reports on the basis of personal interviews with Simon and Lindblom that this difference was revealed in the tension between Lasswell and Lindblom when the two served as consultants to the Cornell University Vicos field experiment in Peru (see Lasswell and McDougal 1992: 894–895, 1109–1114). Although Vicos combined aspects of institutional "profiling" with field experimentation, Lindblom was skeptical about what he saw as Lasswell's "synoptic" approach to planning the Vicos community, just as Hayek (1945) was skeptical about the use of professional-scientific knowledge for government planning. In some respects, Lindblom and Cohen's *Usable Knowledge: Social Science and Social Problem Solving* (1979) is a skeptical successor to Hayek (see Hoppe 1999), who was a professor at Chicago when Lindblom was completing his PhD in economics.

3.10 The Circuitry of Decisional Functions

Lasswell's decisional functionalism has other characteristics that have been dismissed or ignored by critics who incorrectly assert that Lasswell's decision model is linear or mono-cyclical (for a review, see Jann and Wegrich 2007). Instead, Lasswell's decision process is best seen as a complex circuit, much as Dewey defined his reflex arc as an organic circuit of stimuli, responses, and purposes. In Lasswell's circuit, the seven major functions proceed forward, backward, laterally, and diagonally, while within each function are identical subfunctions that also may move forward, backward, laterally, and diagonally. Given that the major functions and subfunctions have *intelligence* at the center of the circuit, where there are more inter-function connections, the entire set of complex decisions forms a circuitry of which intelligence is central to other functions (Figure 2).[24]

[24] The functions and subfunctions are analogous to a wheels-within-a-wheel structure.

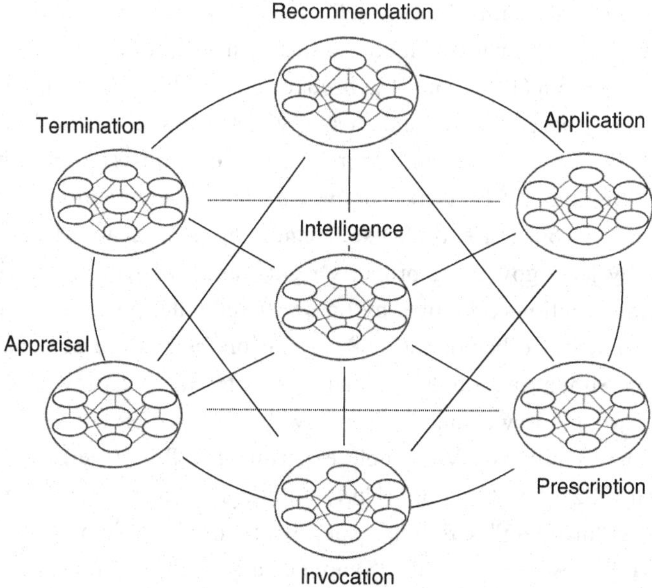

Figure 2 Circuitry of decision processes

Figure 2 illustrates Lasswell's description of the decision process (1956a: 14–15) which may be represented as a complex circuit. Overall, the entire arrangement is not linear but cyclical. "Every agency of government is involved in varying degree with every function; and ... all the component parts of American society are expected to express themselves at least through the electorate." When functions are relatively stable in their interactions, they tend to display cyclical fluctuations and "functional interactions occur among (and within) the participants." Using the example of cycles of urban reform and corruption, Lasswell recognizes that:

> [C]ycles are rarely if ever "perfect"; they do not re-establish the original state of affairs completely. Political fluctuations are structural as well as cyclical; new patterns of interaction emerge and become relatively stable, and the level of conformity between prescription and conduct may be higher or lower than it was before. (Lasswell 1956b: 97).

4 Functionalism and Policy Change

Lasswell's functionalism is based on a pragmatist methodology and philosophy of science, one that rejects positivist conceptions of cause as a correspondence between dual entities of thought and fact, contemplation and action (Ascher and Hirschfelder-Ascher 2004: 7). Kaplan and Lasswell insisted on unity, not dualism, when they chose the "configurative" approach to decisions as an expression of the unity of contemplation and action (Lasswell and Kaplan 1950: xxvi–xxvii).

4.1 Practical Reasoning

Lasswell's views of functional explanation were linked to Dewey and the pragmatists, particularly to practical reasoning. A key to Dewey's thought (1933/1991, 1938/1982) is his definition of practical reasoning as the "general method of intelligence." Practical reasoning is reasoning with a purpose. Lasswell's *decisional functions* are specific categories of practical reasoning that he used to characterize the decision process. As we have seen, the term *decisional function* refers to a category or class of policy decisions or choices. The decisional function of intelligence, following Dewey, is a category of decisions directed toward the attainment of the scope-value of enlightenment. In general, the function of a decision is the *effect* it has on the achievement of political, economic, and moral values such as the eight scope-values identified by Lasswell and Kaplan (1950). Scope-values are ends, while base-values are means to ends.

4.2 The Problem Orientation

Decisional functions may be seen as requisites of the kind elaborated by one of the founders of structural-functionalist theory, Talcott Parsons (1949).[25] For example, the function or purpose achieved by decisions performed under the intelligence function is to obtain knowledge by clarifying goals, describing trends, analyzing conditions that affect the direction and magnitude of trends, forecasting future developments, and inventing, evaluating, and selecting policy alternatives (McDougall et al. 1972). The performance of the intelligence function is identical to what Lasswell called the *problem orientation*. What was then meant by the intelligence function was detailed in similar analytical writings in policy analysis that originate in applied mathematics, operations research, and applied microeconomics, for example, Quade (1989) and Weimer and Vining (2015). The essential difference, however, is that economics is proximally *ex ante*, while Lasswell's intelligence function is a more ambitious and bold form of prospective reasoning. It seeks answers about potential future configurations of political power and economic and technological growth that may enable and constrain the achievement of scope-values. Whereas Lasswell's preferred method was the "developmental

[25] Following Parsons (1949), Lasswell's theoretical orientation resembles structural functionalism. The difference is that decisional functions are contextual. They are related to what Lasswell calls "ends-in-view" (Lasswell 1948), rather than functions of the social system.

construct," which permits long-term forecasts (Lasswell 1941; also see Ascher 1978), economists and operations researchers tend to favor far shorter time horizons.

Performance of the intelligence function is necessary for the accomplishment of other decisional functions, because knowledge or even enlightenment is required for promoting, prescribing, invoking, applying, appraising, and terminating policies. Thus, the completion of any two-step, three-step, or *n*-step process of decisional functions, including those that involve decisional subfunctions (Figure 2), requires the performance of decisions associated with the intelligence function.[26] It is important to note that what was described earlier as the *decision process* presupposes that decision makers are the holders of legitimate (constitutive) political power (McDougal et al. 1967). By contrast, the social process that runs parallel to the technical decision process involves, among other things, participation of individuals and groups with multiple perspectives. The social process is the context in which decision processes function, or what Bower (1968: ch. 3) describes with notable clarity as "a technical process embedded in a social process."

4.3 Abduction and Practical Inference

Apart from its basis in functionalist theory, an essential logical feature of pragmatism is abduction, or what Peirce called the "method of hypothesis." Applied to the area of public policy, abduction resembles the process of making a practical inference. Figures 3(a) and 3(b) show how practical inferences provide teleological explanations of individual and collective actions.[27]

However, in the first practical inference, 3(a), D may not achieve *a*, and for this reason, the inference cannot be justified by a universal covering law (nomic connection), as would be the case if it were a deductive-nomological explanation. Similarly, in the second practical inference, 3(b), O may not achieve *a* because there is no nomic connection or universal covering law. The first practical inference is a quasi-causal explanation and the second is a quasi-teleological explanation (von Wright 1971: 96–98). The term *quasi*, as used here, refers to the absence of a nomic connection such as Alfred Marshall's law of diminishing utility of money, or Avogadro's law of gases.

[26] The word "seems" is used because Lasswell does not specify the length of a sequence of functions. A number of observers (e.g., Brunner 1991) have also noted that the intelligence function is a subfunction of all other decisional functions. Indeed, each of the seven decisional functions has seven decisional subfunctions (Figure 2).

[27] This is among the main reasons that Lasswell was not a logical positivist (see Ascher and Hirschfelder-Ascher 2004: 7–9).

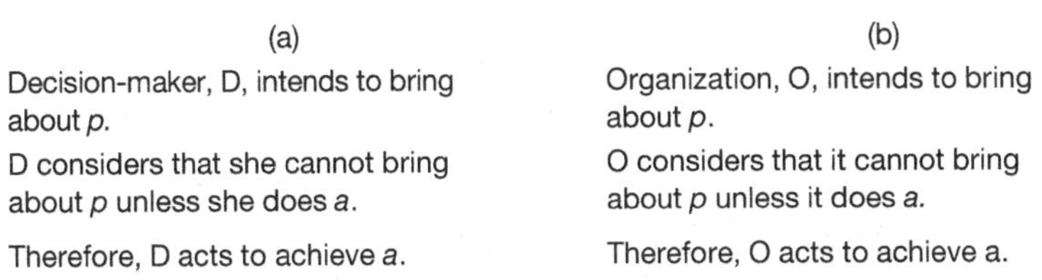

(a)	(b)
Decision-maker, D, intends to bring about *p*.	Organization, O, intends to bring about *p*.
D considers that she cannot bring about *p* unless she does *a*.	O considers that it cannot bring about *p* unless it does *a*.
Therefore, D acts to achieve *a*.	Therefore, O acts to achieve a.

Figure 3 Individual and collective teleological explanations

These two forms of explanation do not conform to the requirements of deductive-nomological explanation, which is the favored mode of explanation in positivist social science. However, what is important is not whether a form of explanation conforms (or not) to explanation in the natural sciences, but whether a form of explanation that is used in the social and behavioral sciences helps one understand why individual and collective actions occur. Conformity to explanation in physics or chemistry is beside the point, because quasi-causal and quasi-teleological explanations enlarge our capacity to understand policy choices.

4.4 Volitional Pragmatism

Daniel Bromley (2006), a gifted interpreter of pragmatism and its applicability to public policy, has developed a theory of volitional pragmatism that builds on earlier ideas of John Dewey and Addison Moore (1910). Bromley shows how abductive reasoning may be used to explain inferences based on practical reasoning (the practical syllogism). Consider again the example of a person turning on a light switch: the person "flips the light switch because he desires that the room be lighted. This desire for a future state (a particular outcome) is the reason for the choice, while the cause is that he flipped the light switch. The flipping of the switch is merely a necessary though quite uninteresting step in the process that starts with reason, entails a causal sequence, and ends with a desired outcome" (Bromley 2006: 7). This example illustrates the reasoning employed by Dewey in the reflex arc.

The example of the light switch also illustrates Lasswell's "maximization postulate." The postulate that "living forms are predisposed to complete acts in ways that are perceived to leave the actor better off than if he had completed them differently" is a form of practical reasoning. The person flips the light switch in order to achieve a future state, a lighted room, which would not have occurred if the switch had not been flipped. Similarly, policy makers may decide to create a future state, an enlightened electorate. The enlightened electorate follows a decision to analyze and disseminate intelligence, specifically, information about the benefits of civic education for voting and other forms of political participation. The use of information about the causal mechanism linking civic education and political participation is a necessary step in the process that begins with the desire for an enlightened electorate, entails the process specified in the causal mechanism, and ends with the desired outcome, an enlightened electorate. It is the future state, an enlightened electorate, which is the reason for the decision, while the act of gathering, processing, and disseminating information is the cause.[28]

Another way to view Lasswell's maximization postulate is to recognize that it involves two kinds of premises: *volitional premises* and *epistemic premises* (Bromley 2006: 14–15; see also Bromley 2008). A volitional premise is a proposition concerning an end of action, or what Lasswell and Kaplan call a goal value. By contrast, an epistemic premise refers to a type of knowledge. Knowledge, which we may define as plausibly true belief, provides the ingredients of the causal mechanism that helps realize the volitional premise. Significantly, this conceptualization avoids the concern expressed by Brunner (1991) that the maximization postulate might be misinterpreted as a form of Paretian expected utility, which was not Lasswell's intention. On the contrary, a pragmatist conception of policy holds that:

> [N]ew public policy starts with a consideration of particular desired outcomes in the future (the volitional premise). The epistemic premise – of the form, "If Y then X" – connects the desired outcome (Y) with the necessary action (X) to achieve that outcome . . . the epistemic premise is both a prediction and a prescription. (Bromley 2006: 15)

Abductive reasoning originated with Peirce, who passed the concept down to Dewey and other doctoral students in a class in logic and scientific method at Johns Hopkins. Although Dewey did not use the concept in his writings, he did discuss abduction without naming it so. In *Logic: The Theory of Inquiry* (1938), he presents a five-step process of inquiry in which the first stage is much like abduction.[29] As Lasswell and Kaplan note (1950: xxv):

> Inquiry has not only a creative role in the formation of policy . . . but also an instrumental role in implementing policy. Thus, the purport of inquiry is not necessarily "theoretical" rather than "practical": both manipulative and contemplative standpoints may be adopted.

[28] This is the "activity theory of causation" that Cook and Campbell (1979: 25–28) use to explain the nature of causation in field experiments and quasi-experiments.

[29] Despite internal conflicts surrounding the definition of pragmatism (e.g., James's pragmatism and Peirce's pragmaticism), Dewey's doctrine of instrumentalism parallels Peirce's pragmatic maxim: "Consider what effects, that might conceivably have practical bearings, we conceive the object of our conception to have. Then, our conception of these effects is the whole of our conception of the object."

They go on to emphasize that inquiry begins with Dewey's *problem situation*, which is identical to the *indeterminate situation* or *surprise* that triggers Peirce's abduction. Bromley (2006), stressing that abduction is a basic feature of the epistemological theory of pragmatism, coins the term *volitional pragmatism*, which refers to the ways that individuals deploy reasons to justify their decisions.

Functional decision theory supplies a rich and variegated representation of policy making. Although the decision process is temporally ordered, and for this reason meets one of several requirements of a causal or quasi-causal mechanism (see Gerring 2010), a theory is needed to explain the operation of the causal mechanism. Although the maximization postulate relates act meanings to subsequent behavior, some argue that this relation is not causal (e.g., Brown 2002). If this were true, Jenkins-Smith and Sabatier (1993) might be correct that Lasswell's decision model is in fact a "heuristic," a means of discovering hypotheses but not of testing and possibly corroborating them. Hence, the "stages heuristic" may not actually permit explanations of how one stage leads to another; it is not a causal model with a clearly defined *explanandum* ("dependent variable") and *explanans* ("independent variable"). In this context, Jann and Wegrich (2007: 57) argue that the "stages heuristic" is inadequate as a theory to explain the policy-making process.

In addressing this criticism, it is essential to recognize that Lasswell's *decisional functionalism* affirms that purposeful behaviors and other subjectively meaningful acts provide an explanation of decisions and their effects. For example, the purpose (or function) of policy invocation and application – what we now might call policy implementation – may be said to enable individuals and groups to achieve values of power and skill. As Brown (2002: 290) explains, functionalism is a form of qualitative methodology, a way to represent and understand act meanings. We understand act meanings when we understand the meaning of acts to participants in the policy-making process, as distinguished from understandings derived from our own or someone else's reconstructions of those acts.[30]

For Lasswell, one source of the concept of decision was emerging functionalist theories in biology and the social sciences (McDougal et al. 1967: 258 and note 6), especially the functionalist social and psychological theories of Dewey and other pragmatists (Ascher and Hirschfelder-Ascher 2004). Functionalism

[30] Colebatch (2002: 125) provides a good example of the logical reconstruction of act meanings of participants in the policy-making process when he observes that the "scientific" model of policy making is not so much an accurate theory as an idealistic view of how people think policy should be made.

explains variations in outcomes of decisions by referring to antecedent purposes, aims, or functions. Although political science and other social science disciplines have preferred deductive-nomological and inductive-statistical models of explanation rather than functional explanations, it is noteworthy that functional models of explanation have recently been productively resurrected in the area of governance and public policy (Peters and Pierre 2016: vii–viii). However, the functional model of decision-making was perhaps destined to be viewed as a mere "heuristic," because traditionally functionalism has been associated with discovering hypotheses through a heuristic process of discovery (the so-called context of discovery), rather than a process of testing hypotheses (the so-called context of justification). Until relatively recently, only the latter has been seen as genuinely theoretical.[31]

However, Lasswell's decisional functionalism may be regarded as a testable theory in the context of justification. To be sure, Brown (2002: 290) contends that functional explanations are not causal, because they are based on "an understanding of the way in which individuals actually relate to the world from their own standpoint (as best this can be determined) rather than an understanding of their conduct as grasped via conceptual categories imposed on or constraints external to that conduct." However, as Arnold Levison and others (following Max Weber) have argued, qualitative explanations based on interpretive understanding complement causal explanations based on overt actions and other physical processes (Levison 1966).[32] Act meanings and other processes of practical reasoning, including Lasswell's maximization postulate, may be regarded as quasi-causal because they explain behavior without resorting to a covering law or nomic connection (von Wright 1971: 91–103). Quasi-causal explanations provide explanations in their own right, explanations that complement explanations based on "external" economic and social factors such as income, wealth, and social status. Indeed, functional explanations based on interpretive understanding may complement deductive-nomological, inductive-statistical, and practical relevance modes of explanation explicated by Wesley Salmon (1984) in his authoritative treatise on scientific explanation. In short, if the central tasks of theory are explanation and prediction, Lasswell's decisional functionalism qualifies as a theory,

[31] Critics of the distinction no longer see the two contexts as mutually exclusive. They have reformulated the mutually exclusive dichotomy between contexts of discovery and justification proposed by Hans Reichenbach in 1938.

[32] Levison's analysis of Karl Hempel's critique of Max Weber contends that Hempel (1959) overlooked narrative evidence showing that Weber did not reject causality. Weber argued instead that a causal explanation required initial conditions that were based both on external (physical) factors and on subjective ones (interpretive understanding). This is the complementarity thesis, which holds that interpretive and causal explanations are compatible and mutually supportive.

although explanation and prediction need not be symmetrical. A sound explanation is not necessary for a sound prediction.

Because functional explanations are teleological explanations, they are goal-directed. Although the weight of scholarly opinion has been skeptical of the use of functional explanations in science (Couch 2011), Ernest Nagel, in *The Structure of Science: Problems in the Logic of Scientific Explanation* (Nagel 1968: 403–405), has argued such explanations can be represented without resort to teleology.

> The function of **A** in a system **S** with organization **C** is to enable **S** in environment **E** to engage in process **P**.

This statement can be expanded into a causal explanation that is not based on purpose or teleology (Nagel 1968: 403; von Wright 1971: 141–142):

> A system **S** with organization **C** in environment **E** engages in process **P**.
> If **S** with organization **C** in environment **E** does not have **A**, then **S** does not engage in process **P**.

The expansion into a causal explanation can be illustrated with an example from science and technology policy (Bimber 1998: 202–225):

> The function of the Office of Technology Assessment (OTA) of the U.S. Congress, which is organized as a bicameral legislature in a democratic environment, is to enable elected members of Congress to engage in legislative processes involving complex issues of science and technology. In democratically elected legislatures, members engage in the legislative process, which is organized in functions that include intelligence, promotion, prescription, invocation, application, termination, and appraisal. If a democratically elected legislature does not have an agency that performs economic and social technology assessments, it will not be able to engage effectively in the legislative process involving complex science and technology issues.[33]

Arguably, this is a deductive-nomological explanation with a lawful regularity, **L**, a set of initial conditions, **C1** and **C2** (the *explanans* and *explanandum*), and the conclusion: *Democratically elected legislatures that do not have an agency that performs technology assessments, or their functional equivalent, will not be able to engage effectively in the legislative process involving complex science and technology issues.* Although the explanation may appear obvious, it is nevertheless

[33] The OTA was abolished by act of the US Congress on September 29, 1995, on grounds that its functions could be performed by other agencies. Although the Library of Congress, the Office of Management and Budget, and the US General Accounting (now Accountability) Office perform technology assessments, they do so without the significant expertise of what was a large, specialized staff of 143 employees.

a deductive-nomological explanation of the type put forth by Nagel (1968) and Hempel (1965) and seemingly preferred by critics of Lasswell's "stages heuristic."

The deductive-nomological model is but one type of causal explanation. Lasswell's decisional functionalism also provides explanations, and testable theories and hypotheses, which do not conform to the deductive-nomological model. For example, in *A Pre-View of Policy Sciences* (1971: 86–100), Lasswell identifies attributes of information used to evaluate the performance of all decisional functions. These attribute variables could form the basis of a "concatenated" or "factor" theory, which Kaplan (1964: 298) contrasts with theories of the deductive or "law" type. One hypothesis is that governments that perform the intelligence function are more likely to achieve the value of enlightenment when the information produced has the attributes of dependability, comprehensiveness, selectivity, creativity, and openness (see also McDougal et al. 1972).[34] This and other hypotheses appear just as testable, causally relevant, and falsifiable as do those derived from alternative theoretical frameworks such as the advocacy coalition framework (ACF), which is also a concatenated or factor-type theory.

5 The Unity of Knowledge and Policy

As we have seen, the maximization postulate is an extension of practical reasoning and the pragmatist theory of action.[35] An essential logical feature of pragmatism is abduction, or what Peirce called the "method of hypothesis," a feature that helps explain policies in terms of the future purposes of action.[36] Abductive reasoning is an integral part of decisional functionalism and the explanation of policy change.

5.1 Pragmatism and the Maximization Postulate

Lasswell's maximization postulate is an extension of the theory of action of James, Peirce, and Dewey.[37] Because the links between Lasswell's functional theory of decision processes and pragmatism were not well documented, critics

---

[34] Carol Weiss (1979), a major producer of work on knowledge use by policy makers, focused on enlightenment as a consequence of the use of social science knowledge. As editor of the journal (*Science Communication*) in which Sabatier's first paper on the ACF was published, I was particularly concerned that the ACF address Weiss's enlightenment function.

[35] Lasswell's decisional functionalism provides an explanation of why policy research (the intelligence function) may serve the enlightenment function of social research documented by Carol Weiss (1979).

[36] This is one of the reasons that Lasswell was not a logical positivist (see Ascher and Hirschfelder-Ascher 2004).

[37] As a doctoral student, Dewey worked with Peirce at Johns Hopkins in the 1890s. The two eventually disagreed about the nature of pragmatism, with Peirce coining the term "pragmaticism" to distinguish his point of view from James's pragmatism and Dewey's instrumentalism. This history is treated by Louis Menand in *The Metaphysical Club* (2001: 357–361).

of the "stages heuristic" could not achieve a proper understanding of Lasswell's theory of the decision process. Abductive explanations are inferences based on the practical syllogism, which like all syllogisms has three elements or premises. Consider again the example of a person turning on a light switch: The person "flips the light switch because he desires that the room be lighted. This desire for a future state (a particular outcome) is the reason for the choice, while the cause is that he flipped the light switch. The flipping of the switch is merely a necessary though quite uninteresting step in the process that starts with reason, entails a causal sequence, and ends with a desired outcome" (Bromley 2006: 7).

The case of the light switch helps to explicate Lasswell's maximization postulate: "living forms are predisposed to complete acts in ways that are perceived to leave the actor better off than if he had completed them differently." It is important to stress that the postulate is a form of practical reasoning. The person flips the light switch in order to achieve a future state, a lighted room, which would not have occurred if the switch had not been flipped. Similarly, policy makers may decide to create a future state, an enlightened electorate. An enlightened electorate, the value, follows the decision to gather, analyze, and disseminate intelligence, specifically, information about how to mount civic education programs that will generate greater political participation. The use of information about the causal mechanism linking civic education and political participation is a necessary step in the process that begins with the desire for an enlightened electorate, entails the sequence specified in the causal mechanism, and ends with the desired outcome, an enlightened electorate. It is the future state, an enlightened electorate, which is the reason for the decision, while the act of gathering, processing, and disseminating information is the quasi-cause.[38]

Another way to view Lasswell's postulate, although he did not do so, is to recognize that it involves two kinds of premises: *volitional premises* and *epistemic premises* (Bromley 2006: 14–15; see also Bromley 2008). A volitional premise is a proposition concerning an end of action, while an epistemic premise refers to types of knowledge. Knowledge, defined as plausibly true belief, provides the ingredients of the causal mechanism that helps to realize the volitional premise. Significantly, this conceptualization

[38] It is a quasi-cause because there is no covering law or nomic connection from which effects can be deduced. This is the "activity theory of causation" that Cook and Campbell (1979: 25–28) use to explain the nature of causation underlying experimental policy interventions. They draw on Collingwood (1940), von Wright (1971), and other advocates of qualitative methodology to explain the nature of causality in policy experimentation. Dewey held essentially the same view.

avoids the concern expressed by Brunner (1991) that the maximization postulate might be misinterpreted as a form of Paretian expected utility, which was not Lasswell's intention. On the contrary, a pragmatist conception of policy holds that:

> [N]ew public policy starts with a consideration of particular desired outcomes in the future (the volitional premise). The epistemic premise – of the form, "If Y then X" – connects the desired outcome (Y) with the necessary action (X) to achieve that outcome . . . the epistemic premise is both a prediction and a prescription. (Bromley 2006: 15)

Abductive reasoning originated with Peirce, who reportedly passed the concept down to Dewey and other students (including Thorstein Veblen, who also taught at Chicago) in a class in logic and scientific method at Johns Hopkins.

Dewey used the concept of abduction, without naming it so. In *Logic: The Theory of Inquiry* (1938/1982), he presents a five-step process of inquiry in which the first stage, much like Bromley's state of surprise, is genuine doubt. This same state of doubt also prompted inquiry for other pragmatists, including Peirce, who linked it to abduction. Without using the term *abduction*, Dewey referred to the doubt as a "problem situation," which present-day policy scholars have referred to both as a diffuse set of worries that precedes efforts to define problems (Rein and White 1977) and as an "ill structured" problem (Simon 1973; Mitroff 1974; Dunn 2018: ch. 3). In contrast to what Kaplan (1964: 43) sees as the vulgar notion that pragmatism is merely about applying theory to practice, the basic proposition of pragmatism is that "knowledge is an instrument or organ of successful action" (Menand 1997: xii).[39] Bromley (2006) stresses that abduction is a basic feature of the epistemological theory of pragmatism, a theory he aptly calls *volitional pragmatism*, because it refers to the ways that individuals deploy reasons to justify their decisions.

5.2 The Pragmatist Maxim and the Associational Fallacy

The difference between the meanings of practical and pragmatic can be clarified by considering Peirce's pragmatist maxim: "Consider what effects, which might conceivably have practical bearings, we conceive the object of our conception to have. Then, our conception of those effects is the whole of our conception of the object" (Peirce 1877: 26–49). Given this meaning of

[39] Despite internal conflicts surrounding the definition of pragmatism (e.g., James's pragmatism and Peirce's pragmaticism), Dewey's doctrine of instrumentalism parallels Peirce's pragmatic maxim, although the latter was about meaning and not causation, per se:"

pragmatism, Lasswell was an unlikely proponent of purely analytical-technical decision processes. For Lasswell, it is *social processes* that define the context in which *technical processes* occur. Each part of the process has "practical bearings" that are meaningful together, but not alone. By focusing on social and analytical-technical processes as a unity, policy scientists adopt what Lasswell called a *contextual orientation* toward decision processes. To adopt a contextual orientation is to identify ways that decisions affect and are affected by elements of the social process, elements that include participants, perspectives, situations, values, strategies, outcomes, and effects (Lasswell 1971: 15–17). For this reason, to paraphrase Lasswell's virtual mantra, the policy sciences yield knowledge *of* and *in* the policy-making process.

Although it may not be readily evident, the dictum is an expression of both Lasswell's *contextual orientation* and the *pragmatist maxim.* The former is intended to link decision processes and social processes. Otherwise, technical and social processes, if treated as a duality, are prone to the commission of an associational fallacy. An associational fallacy is a faulty inference that one process is associated with another process when it is not. The fallacy is that analytical-technical processes, simply because they are logically similar to policy making as a social process, are mutually relevant.

The associational fallacy, or the fallacy of relevance by association, is similar to guilt by association, where person B is guilty by association with person C, because both are engaged in fleeing the scene of a crime, A, notwithstanding that B is escaping arrest, while C is avoiding harm at the hands of a criminal. In public policy, the associational fallacy has the same form. The (social) process of policy making (B) and the (technical) process of policy analysis (C) are associated with a common function, for example, the choice of a policy (A). This is the fallacy of relevance by association. The process of choosing a policy (A) is a property of policy making (B); the process of choice (A) is also a property of policy analysis (C), for example, by using cost-benefit analysis to choose a policy with net efficiency improvement.

Therefore, the (technical) process of policy analysis (B) and the (social) process of policy making (C) appear to be mutually relevant by association because both involve choice (A). For example, a cost-benefit analysis may be performed by a university research team to recommend the adoption of a health care program after summing and subtracting total costs from total benefits to obtain net benefits. At the same time, an analysis of political pros and cons may be performed by the staff of a government ministry to choose the same program. Because processes of choice, A, occur in both contexts, B is inferred to be relevant to C by association, when in fact it is not (Figure 4).

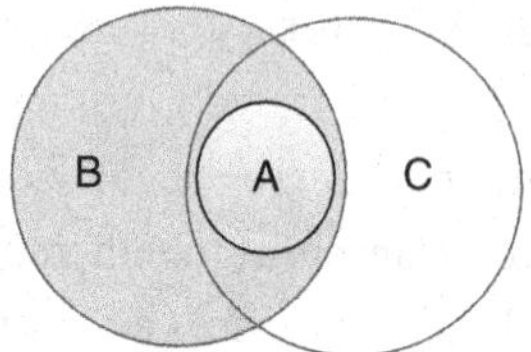

Figure 4 Associational fallacy

The fallacy cannot be resolved unless policy analysts and policy makers actually collaborate on the choice, A, of a policy. Consider again Peirce's pragmatic maxim: "Consider what effects, which might conceivably have practical bearings, we conceive the object of our conception to have. Then, our conception of those effects is the whole of our conception of the object." When the object of our conception is cost-benefit analysis, the practical effects are making a choice between alternatives that is rational because the preferred option has greater net benefits. By contrast, when the object is the analysis of political feasibility in an agency setting, the practical effects are making a choice between alternatives that are most coherent, that is, have the proper (coherent) mix of factors involving efficiency, power, timing, communications, and so on.

The fallacy of policy relevance by association is perhaps the fundamental weakness of policy analysis and one of the reasons policy analysis is often not used by policy makers. Indeed, entire books (e.g., Lindblom and Cohen 1979) have been written about this simple fallacy without calling it that.

To minimize such problems, Lasswell proposed *continuous decision seminars* that link social and technical decision processes in a unity of knowledge and action, theory and practice. The two kinds of processes may have a joint effect with "practical bearings" when they are joined in a common function or purpose (Lasswell 1960), or as Hoppe (1999) puts it, if the process moves from "speaking truth to power" to "making sense together."

6 The Roots of Misinterpretation

Lasswell's death in 1978 was followed by a handful of commemorative essays as well as critiques of his work. Given Lasswell's preeminence, it is surprising that, in the twenty-year period 1978–1998, there was a relative paucity of references to his books, and then only to about one-third of them, primarily in mainstream political science rather than public policy (Eulau and Zlomke 1999). Only later were there critiques of his work on the policy-making process (e.g., Sabatier 1991; Farr, Hacker, and Kazee 2006), as distinct from critiques of his writings on the policy sciences generally (e.g., Tribe

1972). Apart from critics, other policy-oriented political scientists commemorated, defended, or extended Lasswell's work (e.g., Torgerson 1985; Brunner 1991, 1997; DeLeon 1994; Brown 2002; Ascher and Hirschfelder-Ascher 2004). The negligible attention paid to his work on the decision process by mainstream political scientists was no doubt a result of the relative lack of importance of policy studies and policy analysis in political science at that time and today.

However, the main root of misplaced criticism is the lack of understanding that the decision process, along with other aspects of Lasswell's work, is rooted in pragmatism. Because Lasswell's theory of the decision process was based on functional analysis, not on the analysis of stages of activities (although the term *sequence* was regularly used), it is regrettable that it came to be known as the "stages model," "stages heuristic," "stages framework," or "stages metaphor."[40]

The so-called stages model, which assumes a sequential process of decision-making, was developed between 1943 and 1992 by Lasswell and McDougal (1943), Lasswell (1956b), McDougal et al. 1972), and Lasswell and McDougal (1992). The model was subsequently simplified and revised by a number of contributors to literature on what May and Wildavsky (1979) and Jann and Wegrich (2007) call the "policy cycle," a construct that calls attention to the fact (of which Lasswell was aware) that policy making is iterative and nonlinear. Prominent among contributors to work on the policy cycle are Jones (1977), May and Wildavsky (1979), Brewer and DeLeon (1983), DeLeon (1999), and Anderson (2011).

What some now call policy "stages" are in fact (or should be) called Lasswell's *decisional functions*: intelligence, promotion, prescription, invocation, application, termination, and appraisal. The term *decisional function* refers to a category or class of decisions, or choices. For example, the decisional function of intelligence is a class of decisions directed toward the attainment of the value of enlightenment (or knowledge). In general, the function of a decision is the *effect* it has on the achievement of political, economic, and moral values such as the base-values (means) and scope-values (ends) identified by Lasswell and Kaplan in *Power and Society* (1950).

Decisional functions may be seen as functional requisites of the kind elaborated by one of the founders of structural-functionalist theory, Talcott

[40] No attempt is made here to distinguish the various meanings of causality. This would unnecessarily lengthen this Element and burden its flow. Useful sources on these questions include Abraham Kaplan (1964), Georg Henrik von Wright (1971), Wesley Salmon (1984), Donald T. Campbell (1988), and Guido Imbens and Donald Rubin (2015).

Parsons (1949).[41] For example, the function or purpose achieved by decisions performed under the intelligence function is to clarify goals, describe trends, analyze conditions that affect the direction and magnitude of trends, forecast future developments, and invent, evaluate, and select alternatives that may attain goals (McDougall et al. 1972). The performance of the intelligence function is virtually identical to what Lasswell called the *problem orientation*. What was then meant by the intelligence function was detailed later in texts on policy analysis written in areas of applied mathematics, operations research, and applied microeconomics (e.g., Quade 1989; Weimer and Vining 2015), not in texts originating in political science (e.g., Jones 1977; Anderson 2011).

Performance of the intelligence function is necessary for the accomplishment of other decisional functions: promotion, prescription, invocation, application, appraisal, and termination. The completion of any two-step, three-step, or *n*-step sequence of decisional functions seems to require the successful completion of the intelligence function.[42] It is important to note that what has been described as the *decision process* presupposes that decision makers are the holders of legitimate (constitutive) political power (McDougal et al. 1967). By contrast, the social process involves, among other things, participation in different policy arenas of individuals and groups with multiple perspectives. The social process provides the context of decision processes, the social process in which technical processes are embedded.

Many of the most important criticisms of the stages model are provided in articles by Sabatier (1988, 1991), a book chapter by Jenkins-Smith and Sabatier (1993), the introductory chapter of Sabatier's widely used edited volume, *Theories of the Policy Process* (1999, 2006), and Auer (2007). Its proponents, in the course of affirming the overall analytical viability and practical utility of the stages model (e.g., DeLeon 1988, 1992; Brunner 1997), have also conceded limitations of the model.

6.1 Criticisms of the Stages Framework

A representative summary of criticisms of the stages model may be found in Jenkins-Smith and Sabatier (1993: 3–4) and DeLeon (1999: 23–24).[43]

41 Lasswell's theoretical orientation resembles structural functionalism, with the difference that a function is a contextual end in view. This is suggested in "The Structure and Function of Communication in Society" (Lasswell 1948).

42 As already noted, Lasswell does not specify the length of a sequence of functions. The intelligence function is an element of all other decisional functions, as well as a separate and independent function.

43 The original criticisms have been restated for purposes of clarity and economy.

6.1.1 Absence of Causality

The stages model is not a causal model because it does not permit predictions or explanations of how one stage leads to another. However, as noted earlier, the type of causality at issue is that which is usually based on a deductive-nomological model characteristic of the natural sciences. As we have seen, what critics refer to as the stages model, when properly viewed in functionalist terms, actually permits quasi-causal explanations that do not depend on a covering law. Moreover, teleological explanations may be converted into explanations based on covering laws.

6.1.2 Heuristic Limitation

The stages model is a heuristic. The term *heuristics*, based on the epistemological distinction between contexts of discovery and justification, refers to activities of discovering concepts, variables, and hypotheses, but not testing them. However, it is incorrect that the Lasswell-McDougal theory of the decision process ignores the distinction between the context of discovery, where hypotheses may be discovered but not tested, and the context of justification, where hypotheses are tested. The distinction between the "context of discovery" and the "context of justification" assumes that the context of discovery is a "non-rational process" that cannot be disciplined by the application of evaluative criteria to knowledge claims. Advocates of the context distinction argue that philosophy of science, and methodology generally, is exclusively concerned with the context of justification. Decisional functionalism goes well beyond heuristics and the context of discovery, however, into the context of justifying knowledge claims and hypotheses. The alleged inability to test hypotheses because there is no theory from which hypotheses might be deduced and operationalized is also incorrect.

6.1.3 Descriptive Inaccuracy

Critics of the stages model argue that it does not provide accurate descriptions of the policies formulated or implemented at each "stage." Although the Lasswell-McDougal functional model, like any general model, does not describe policies associated with each function, Lasswell and Kaplan (1950) and Lasswell (1956b) provide numerous illustrations of decisions made within each function. Lasswell (1956b: 1) cautions that:

> [W]hen we are dealing with activities that display the infinite variations of institutional practice to be found in government, it is important not to lose sight of the forest by becoming preoccupied with naming the trees. We need schemes that, without becoming unwieldy, are more discriminating than the tripartite division of American tradition.

6.1.4 Legalistic-Hierarchical Bias

The stages model is alleged to be legalistic, discouraging analysis of non-legal processes, and hierarchical, because the model makes no provision for bottom-up generative processes. Although the Lasswell-McDougal two-volume work bears the imprint of McDougal the legal scholar – and the original 1932 policy sciences course at Yale was heavily influenced by the theory of legal realism – legal realism is anti-legalistic in its emphasis on the concept of decision. Decisional functionalism also originated in Dewey's functionalism and from the work on decision-making by Barnard and Simon. In any case, the unity of the decision and social processes is neither legalistic nor hierarchical.

Although many of these criticisms have a surface plausibility, a more systematic assessment of their merit suggests that they are largely mistaken. Because the links between Lasswell's model of decision processes and pragmatism were not fully articulated, critics were unable to achieve a proper understanding.

7 Rediscovering Pragmatism

The writings of Lasswell, Kaplan, and McDougal reflect the multiple influences of James, Peirce, Dewey, and other pragmatists. That said, we now wish to draw out the implications of pragmatism for understanding and, where possible, improving the policy sciences.

7.1 Post-Positivist Pragmatism

The Chicago School of Pragmatism developed in the same period as the Vienna School of Logical Positivism (Empiricism). In contrast to the positivists, however, Lasswell and the pragmatists did not believe that knowledge is simply a mirror of presupposed regularities of nature. For this and other reasons, Lasswell was not a logical positivist. Lasswell and his collaborators did not engage in the preemptive rejection of ethics and values in science, as did the early Vienna Circle positivists. There is no independent reality apart from knowers; knowledge claims are neither objective nor subjective. Instead, they are based on objective relativism, a doctrine that affirms that, while knowledge is relative to observers, it cannot be reduced to personal characteristics or to social contexts. Lasswell was not a relativist; nor was he a logical positivist who relied on the correspondence theory of truth to vindicate knowledge claims. Here, the pragmatist's rhetorical question answers itself: is there truth without correspondence to reality? (Rorty 1999: 23–46).

7.2 The Lasswellian Puzzle

What is puzzling is why Lasswell, with the exception of the first several pages of *A Pre-View of Policy Sciences* (1971) and scattered footnotes to pragmatists in collaborative works (e.g., Lasswell and Kaplan 1950; Lasswell and McDougal 1992), did not elaborate on his debt to Dewey and other pragmatists. The answer, perhaps obvious in retrospect, is given in general terms by Darnell Rucker, a former lecturer at the University of Chicago.

> The Chicago pragmatists developed a methodology that gave the social scientists in Chicago and elsewhere a frame of reference, a perspective, and a consciousness of continuity. It was a methodology that could not be erected legitimately into a fixed organon; it did not function to provide ready-made forms or languages to which social problems had to be adapted. If the character of the method were grasped at all, that method had to be used in such a way that the form and language grew out of the problem itself and reflected the peculiarities of that problem. Yet, at the same time, the interrelations among different social problems were retained through a common problematic perspective. (Rucker 1969: 161–162)

In this context, from roughly 1920 to 1938 at Chicago, and then at Yale from 1943 to 1970, the specific frame of reference and perspective was that of functionalism and the analysis of action. As a student and then professor at the University of Chicago, Lasswell was affected by pragmatist philosophers and social scientists, individually and as members of what came to be known as the Chicago School of Pragmatism.[44]

In those years, Lasswell's "cross-disciplinary manifold" (Lasswell 1971a) provided a common perspective and approach that was interdisciplinary, multimethod, and normative, not only in the formal or analytical sense but also in the socio-organizational and institutional sense conveyed by the metaphor of the cross-disciplinary manifold. The manifold was embedded in multidisciplinary spatial structures including the Social Science Research Building at Chicago, where faculty and their projects were mixed and matched to achieve multidisciplinary interaction and social usefulness, or what we now call policy relevance (Bulmer 1984: 196–197). Compare this social-methodological manifold with the spatial organization of the contemporary university, where faculty are sequestered in specialized disciplinary units within university buildings. This spatial organization promotes what Lasswell, in his presidential address at the 1956 American Political Science

[44] Evidence of the intellectual richness of Chicago includes studies of multiple contenders for the title of "school." See, for example, the Chicago schools of pragmatism (Rucker 1969), sociology (Bulmer 1984), and functionalism (Shook and Backe 2001).

Association annual meeting, described in the contemporary university as "a non-communicating aggregate of experts"(1956b: 979). By contrast, he saw the political science department as

> a true center of integration where normative and descriptive frames of reference are simultaneously and continuously applied to the consideration of the policy issues confronting the body politic as a whole over the near, middle and distant ranges of time. The profession [of political science] is advantageously situated therefore to take the lead in a configurative approach to the decision process in society. Where it plays this part, political science is the policy science, par excellence. (Lasswell 1956b: 979)

The cross-disciplinarity established at Chicago served as an influential institutional precedent for the subsequent establishment of the policy sciences. The policy-oriented, contextual, and multiple-method "cross-disciplinary manifold" of Chicago is a virtual replica of the approach to the policy sciences called for later by Lasswell, Kaplan, and McDougal. Indeed, a kind of "proxy policy sciences" was a going concern in Chicago in the 1930s.

In 1938, Lasswell and Gosnell were denied promotion. Earlier, Hutchins had dismantled the philosophy department by replacing a retiring George Herbert Mead with Mortimer Adler, a bright but abrasive opponent of pragmatism and empirical social science research and a proponent of classical philosophy (see Adler 1977).

7.3 The Circuitry of the Decision Process

Lasswell's decision process involves learning by doing. This is why Lasswell (1956a) states that any one of the seven functions may be related to preceding or succeeding functions, or to subfunctions *within* a particular function. While functions are related as a Cartesian product (Figure 3), the intelligence function is the core of all other functions and subfunctions, because the following analytical tasks are prerequisites of the performance of other functions and subfunctions:

- clarification of goals
- description of trends
- analysis of conditions affecting the direction and magnitude of trends
- forecasting future developments
- inventing, evaluating, and selecting policy alternatives.

A very large number of individuals make policy decisions, even in apparently simple contexts (e.g., Barnard's decision to move a light pole). The complexity of this process is best represented as a functional and purpose-driven circuit, not the linear sequence or cycle employed to characterize the decision process in literature on the policy-making process (e.g., May and Wildavsky 1979).

The circuitry of the decision process, like the circuitry of Dewey's reflex arc, follows the pragmatist principle of the unity of knowing and doing. For the pragmatist:

> Knowing and doing are indivisible aspects of the same process, which is the business of adaptation. We learn, in the progressive phase, by doing: we take a piece of acquired knowledge into a concrete situation, and the results we get constitute a new piece of knowledge, which we carry over into our next encounter with our environment. (Menand 1997: xiii–xiv)

Theories of policy making – for example, rational choice theory or the theory of partisan mutual adjustment – convey knowledge about policy making. For Lasswell and other pragmatists, however, theories (and observations) are not mental copies of a reality external to us; they are instruments of successful (or unsuccessful) action. The principle of the unity of knowing and doing implies that we will fail if we unwittingly adopt the correspondence theory of truth and "scientific realism" by hypostatizing knowledge and embalming it in textbooks and manuals of policy analysis (see Menand 1997: xxiv).

Critics of the so-called stages heuristic have not had access to Lasswell's original writings and, hence, have not been able to appreciate the organized complexity that arises from decisional functionalism. Fortunately, in the field of governance, which is part of the policy sciences, there has been a turn toward functionalism. Peters's and Pierre's *Comparative Governance: Rediscovering the Functional Dimension of Governing* (2016) is a leading example. Critics who appear to call for a single mode of explanation based on deductive-nomological or even hypothetical-deductive reasoning, have largely ignored functionalist explanations. However, functionalist explanations such as those based on Lasswell's "maximization postulate" are useful and appropriate because they are helpful in understanding policy making. Functionalists, rather than seeking to conform to positivist standards of the natural sciences (often as a way to legitimize social science research), appear to be closer to the nature and aims of the social sciences.

One of the most practically important aspects of the policy sciences is the link between pragmatism and functionalism. If Dewey approached almost every problem in terms of the reflex arc and the functional process of teleologically triggered stimulus and response, so did Lasswell approach almost every problem in terms of functional processes of politics (Lasswell 1938), communications (Lasswell 1948), psychology (Lasswell 1960; see Ascher and Hirschfelder-Ascher 2004: 13–14), and the decision process (Lasswell

1956a). Functionalism is one of the keys to understanding his problem-oriented, contextual, multimethod, and normative approach to the policy sciences.

From an epistemological standpoint, it is incorrect that functionalist theory ignores the distinction between the context of discovery, where hypotheses may be discovered but not tested, and the context of hypothesis testing and justification. The distinction between the "context of discovery" and the "context of justification" assumes that the context of discovery is a "non-rational process, a leap of insight that cannot be captured in specific instructions. Justification, by contrast, is a systematic process of applying evaluative criteria to knowledge claims" (Schickore and Steinle 2006: 1–2).

Decisional functionalism, however, goes well beyond heuristics and the context of discovery into the context of justification through testing hypotheses derived from functionalist theory. Indeed, the theory of decisional functionalism permits a range of arguably legitimate explanations that von Wright (1971: 74–83), in his treatise on positivist and non-positivist inquiry, calls quasi-causal and quasi-teleological explanations. What makes either form of explanation "quasi" is the absence of a classical deductive-nomological premise or law, as in classical views of the natural sciences.

7.4 Abductive Reasoning and "Wicked" Problems

By treating indeterminate situations as ordinary and ubiquitous aspects of inquiry, as part of the process of learning and adaptation, what are known as "wicked" problems (Churchman 1967; Webber and Rittel 1974) or ill-structured problems (Simon 1973; Mitroff 1974) may be seen as routine and even uninteresting features of policy analysis and planning. The investigation of indeterminate situations that give rise to diffuse worries, doubts, or surprises appears to be a normal aspect of the process of problem solving (Figure 5). What Dewey meant by a *problem situation* is simply an indeterminate set of conditions that trigger efforts to formulate a *problem*.

In the 1880s, Dewey was Peirce's student at Johns Hopkins, where Dewey must have been introduced to the process of abductive reasoning:

> [A]bduction starts when particular circumstances and events are encountered and we find ourselves in need of an explanation . . . That is, human action is animated, ab initio, by doubt or surprise. Peirce talked of the "irritation of doubt." . . . The essential purpose of abduction is the production of belief about certain events. To quote from Charles Sanders Peirce, "the action of thought is excited by the irritation of doubt, and ceases when belief is attained; so that the production of belief is the sole function of thought." (Peirce 1977/1977: 14–15; Bromley 2006: 23–24)

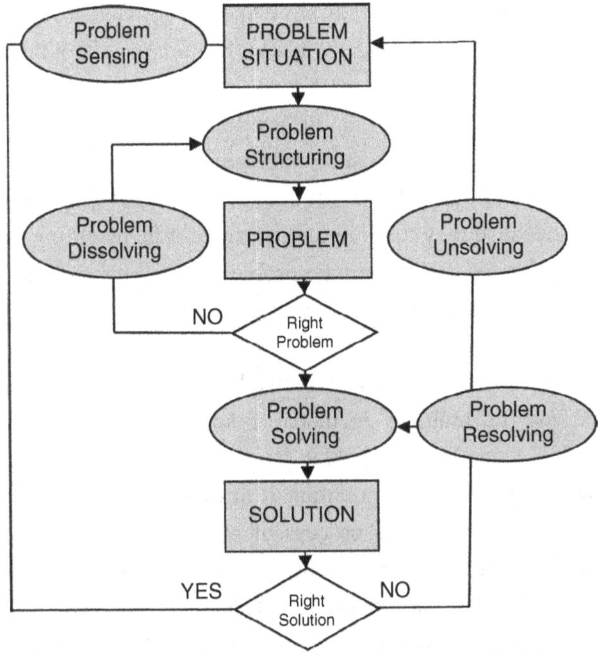

Figure 5 The process of problem structuring

In public policy, the indeterminacy of problem situations produces *surprises, unanticipated events*, or *anomalies* for which there is no apparent explanation. Indeed, nearly all problem situations are what policy methodologists Rein and White (1977: 262) call "diffuse worries and inchoate signs of stress."[45] As Herbert Simon (1973) has written, ill structured problems ([*sic.*] *problem situations*) become structured (or "tamed") in the course of solving them. For Simon, a student of pragmatist social scientists at the University of Chicago, ill-structured problems are coextensive with Dewey's problem situations.

The indeterminacy of knowledge occurs frequently in public policy analysis, sometimes in simple situations where we attempt to deal with omitted variable bias, and at other times when situations are complex due to the interactions of disputed social values and presumed or unknown causally relevant variables, for example, the choice of options to mitigate global warming. Pragmatist Russell Ackoff points out that "[p]roblems are

[45] Dewey was aware of the logical trap of relativism. For this reason, he was no epistemological relativist. Opposed to dogmatic uses of the term *truth*, he redefined the concept, critically and reflectively, as "warranted assertibility," a concept that has much in common with Jürgen Habermas's "truth-redeeming validity claims" and Stephen Toulmin's "substantial arguments," as opposed to deductive ones. In this context, pragmatists such as Abraham Kaplan (1966), stressing the pragmatist rejection of dualities, use Dewey's term *objective relativism*.

elements of problem situations that have been abstracted from these situations through analysis" (Ackoff 1974b: 21). Problems are not "out there" in the world, disembodied from human experience, waiting to be discovered, like Columbus discovered America. Policy problems do not exist apart from the policy makers and citizens who sense and structure them. There are problem situations (Lasswell and McGregor 1992: II:1135–1136) that are indeterminate because they involve unsettling beliefs, troubling doubts, and disconcerting surprises. Indeterminate problem situations are not unusual in science or in policy; they are ordinary and may be expected as a matter of course.

To deal with problem situations, Lasswell and other Chicago pragmatists proposed the use of multiple methods to identify contexts of meaning. "The inference is that if goal variables are to be related to concrete circumstances [or contexts] some interpretation is always necessary" (Lasswell and McDougal 1992: II, 1135). The process of problem structuring or problem definition does not begin with problems, but with problem situations. In this context, Bromley (2008) contrasts standard inductive and deductive reasoning with the abductive reasoning of pragmatists, in order to show how each responds to indeterminate situations and surprises: Can it be true that the homicide rate is related to the fact that in the United States, the number of handguns (more than 300 million) is almost equal to the population of 325 million? If the math and science scores of students in poverty-level central cities are excluded from national averages, does the United States actually rank in the top ten of science and math scores in the world? Do planes crash without sufficient runway when there is high humidity and heat?

Problems do not stay solved; they may be *resolved, unsolved*, or *dissolved*, as shown in Figure 5. The terms *problem resolving, problem unsolving*, and *problem dissolving* designate three types of error correction (Ackoff 1974a: 273–279). Although the three terms come from the same root (L. *solvere*, to solve or dissolve), the error-correcting processes to which they refer are different. *Problem resolving* involves the reanalysis of a correctly structured problem to reduce calibration errors. *Problem unsolving*, by contrast, involves the abandonment of a solution based on the wrong formulation of a problem and a return to problem structuring in an attempt to formulate the right problem. Finally, *problem dissolving* involves the abandonment of the wrong formulation of a problem and a return to problem structuring, starting the process anew. Finally, because problems do not stay solved, identifying the right problem may later mean a return to problem sensing and the detection of new worries, signs of stress, and surprises, that is, a new problem situation.

Policy problems are abstractions from problem situations. Information about policy problems typically includes alternative solutions and, if available, the probabilities that each alternative is likely to lead to a solution. If these requirements are met, the problem is usually described as a "tame" or "well-structured" problem. The way a problem is structured governs the identification of solutions, so that a faulty conceptualization may result in serious or even fatal errors. Raiffa (1968: 264), Mitroff and Featheringham (1974), and Mitroff (1974) have described these errors as *formulating the wrong problem* (Type III errors), which they distinguish from statistical errors resulting from setting the confidence limits too high or too low in testing the null hypothesis (Type I and Type II errors).

7.5 Transactional Field Experiments

The process of problem sensing yields unsettled beliefs, doubts, and surprises, followed by processes of "fixing beliefs" by inventing and successfully testing hypotheses. The product of fixing beliefs engenders sufficient trust that the beliefs may become instruments of action. In his William James Lectures at Harvard, Donald T. Campbell, widely regarded as the founder of the field of policy and program evaluation, called for field experimentation to address problem situations in which we are unable to trust our beliefs, problem situations where the difference between doubt and trust lies heavily in favor of doubt. Campbell argued that experiments should be conducted in these indeterminate situations, not in situations where the evolution of practice wisdom creates more or less "fixed beliefs" and a high trust-to-doubt ratio (see, for example, Campbell and Stanley 1963: 6–7).

Cook and Campbell (1979), Campbell (1988), and Shadish, Cook, and Campbell (2002) have characterized field experiments in functionalist and instrumentalist terms, as instances of the activity theory of causation. By extending functionalism to dynamic and adaptive processes of knowledge transactions, experimental and quasi-experimental designs may be employed to create new forms of experiments that recognize self-generating processes of learning and adaptation. In this context, early experiments with a candle were reinterpreted, not as cases of stimulus and response, but as cases of purpose or intention, followed by stimulus and response, knowledge and adaptation. The candle experiment elicits a painful response, followed by new (in this case painfully acquired) knowledge. The results of the experiment are a new piece of knowledge, which is carried over into the next phase of action. Knowledge is not a mirror of a reality external to us, but an instrument of successful action.[46]

[46] Ascher and Hirschfelder-Ascher (2004) point out the connection between postpositivism and fallibilism: "[P]ragmatism already exhibited the insights shared with postpositivism that are

$O_1 \quad O_2\,\mathbf{X}\,O_3 \quad O_4 \quad O_5 \quad O_6\,\mathbf{X}\,O_7 \quad O_8 \quad O_9 \quad O_{10}\,\mathbf{X}\,O_{11}$

$O_1 \quad O_2 \quad O_3 \quad O_4\,\mathbf{X}\,O_5 \quad O_6 \quad O_7 \quad O_8\,\mathbf{X}\,O_9 \quad O_{10} \quad O_{11}$

Figure 6 Switching replications experiment

This is particularly true when the acquisition of knowledge, and its effects on action, is transacted with others. While new beliefs, attitudes, and behaviors are partially captured in policy experiments designed to assess the impact of civic education programs on political participation, many sources of bias result from the very act of experimentation and the use of questionnaires, interviews, and other reactive measures. These sources of bias, ranging from the biases of experimental subjects and experimenters as they transact knowledge from interviews, questionnaires to archives, are well documented in literature on "reactive measures" (see Webb et al. 1966). What is not known is the effects of these biasing transactions on new knowledge that is acquired, adapted, and used for subsequent action in the course of field experiments.

Policy scientists working in the area of evidence-based policy might address this problem by moving beyond randomized policy experiments with pretest-posttest, control group designs to more robust and pragmatist-inspired designs, for example, designs with switching replications (Figure 6). When one group is exposed to the experimental intervention, the other group serves as a control. When the control group later receives the intervention, the original experimental group serves as a control (Shadish et al. 2002: 102–106). The intervention, however, is not a changeless chunk of knowledge and skills such as those introduced in a job-training program, but a dynamic process of knowledge acquisition, response, adaptation, and the acquisition of new knowledge. However, rather than regarding bias as a nuisance only to be controlled, bias may be regarded as an important part of sequential transactions.

The switching replications design remains true to Dewey's experimentalism as the most trustworthy way of knowing, but allows for the likely differential effects of knowledge transactions on outcome measures among members of experimental and control groups. The switching replications design is preferable to the classic randomized pretest-posttest, control group design.

---

crucial for justifying the status of psychodynamic functional theory: the recognition that ultimate certainty is unattainable" (p. 7).

It would be necessary to do the kinds of qualitative interviews that Chicago pragmatists Park and Lasswell used with surveys of unemployed workers and displaced immigrants (Bulmer 1984: 70–71). Park's pragmatist interpretation of the social survey is worth quoting at length. Bulmer (1984: 71), drawing from the University of Chicago archive of Park's field notes, provides a window into the link between survey research and pragmatism.

> [F]acts are through and through imbued with our own practical interests and points of view ... there are no pure facts. James's point that a distinction which does not make a difference to someone, somewhere is not only not worth making, it is not even a fact ... In this sense "pragmatic" would mean that a fact is never quite a fact merely because it is investigated and recorded. It only becomes a fact when it is delivered and delivered to the person to whom it makes a difference. This is what the survey seeks to do.

In 1916, Park's colleague Ernest W. Burgess had already likened the social survey to a method of investigation as well as a form of social activism. "The social survey provides a unique opportunity both for investigation and for social construction, both for the analysis of mental attitudes and for the control of forces in seeming improvement" (Burgess 1916; quoted in Bulmer 1984: 73 n).

Surveys are often employed as parts of time-series experiments designed to make plausible causal inferences about the effects of policies and programs. In such contexts, there are numerous opportunities for bias and other threats to validity (Shadish et al. 2002: 195–196). Interrupted time-series experiments frequently involve policy interventions that are implemented slowly and that diffuse throughout a population; the effects of the intervention are modeled as a gradually diffusing process rather than an intervention with sharp effects. Many effects seem to occur with unpredictable delays that differ among groups over time.

In such situations, it is likely that some part of diffusion times is a result of learning and adaptation, so that the concept of a transactional experiment becomes relevant. A transactional experiment might use a combination of a time-series experiment and communication network analysis. In one design, investigators planned to examine the effects of policy interventions (in this case, information packets with policy-relevant information) at multiple points in time in the policy-making process. However, to investigate knowledge transactions, the density of communications networks and the distribution of network roles were hypothesized to affect beliefs and attitudes toward educational policies. This design might best be described as a transactional experiment.

7.6 Explaining Policy Effectiveness: The Maximization Postulate

Lasswell proposed the use of the "maximization postulate" as a means to explain the effects of changes in goal values – for example, intelligence, wealth, power, or rectitude – on the performance of decisional functions. Much like Dewey's reflex arc, values drive the search for causal mechanisms that may (but not necessarily) make the values achievable. This is what Bromley conceptualizes as volitional and epistemic premises.[47] A volitional premise is an expression of a goal value(s). A volitional premise is a response to a problem situation (an indeterminate situation evoking doubt or surprise), while an epistemic premise is a trusted belief, often in the form of a causal mechanism, that explains as well as justifies why an action should be taken to achieve the goal value(s) in the volitional premise.

7.7 The Unity of Knowledge and Policy

Institutional mechanisms such as Lasswell's continuous decision seminar (Lasswell 1960) are designed to draw together and unite the functions of the decision process and the social process. The latter provides the context that makes decisions relevant, with the term *relevance* applied to decisions that involve the use of evidence to shape public policies. Relevant decisions, in this sense, mitigate the associational fallacy, a form of faulty reasoning based on the assumption that there are strong linkages between the policy sciences, on one hand, and the contexts in which they are designed to be used by policy makers, on the other. Abstract macro-negative assessments of these linkages based on Hayek (1945) or Lindblom and Cohen (1979) fail to recognize the contexts in which policy scientists and policy makers can and sometimes do work in tandem. Indeed, the pragmatic instrumentalism of Dewey and Lasswell may serve as an antidote to the faulty conception of a necessarily blunt or negative role of the policy sciences and correct the disappointing record of schools of public administration and policy in teaching about and seeking to improve the use of scientific evidence in policy making (National Academy of Sciences 2009).

7.8 The Marshallian Inversion

In economics, the tradition of marginal analysis, tradeoffs, and opportunity costs inaugurated by Alfred Marshall in *Principles of Economics* (1890) has promoted a perspective that what makes a discipline scientific is its capacity to

[47] The term *volitional*, when juxtaposed with *epistemic*, can imply that values are not a form of knowledge. Dewey and the pragmatists viewed ethics and values, including the goal of human dignity, as forms of naturalistically acquired knowledge.

discover in nature regularities that confirm hypotheses and theories. From the standpoint of scientific realism, economics yields true statements about economic phenomena because economic theories conform to the world (Hausman 1992: 286–287). Significantly, Lasswell and the pragmatists inverted this perspective: economics and other policy sciences yield true statements because they conceptualize and order the world systematically, knowing that statements about it never fully or unequivocally correspond to presupposed regularities of economic phenomena. To be sure, the policy sciences can pursue truth, human dignity, and democratic values, but without the assurance that knowledge claims can ever achieve the goal of correspondence. The pragmatist principle of objective relativism transcends the dualism of objectivism and relativism.

For pragmatists, beliefs are instruments of action. If beliefs make no difference to an analyst or policy maker, they are not worth retaining. They are not even factual. If concepts, conceptual frameworks, and theories make no difference for contemplation and action, then the pragmatists recommend that we discard them. They are of no consequence.

****

The development of the policy sciences after 1950 is regarded by some as little more than an anachronistic episode in the evolution of the applied social sciences. Given the name *policy* sciences, the bulk of attention has been directed toward the Lasswell-McDougal model of the decision process. Not only has the model of the decision process been misunderstood as a linear "stages heuristic" but the model also has drawn attention away from the conditions underlying Lasswell's achievements and those of his closest collaborators.

First and foremost, these conditions include Lasswell's growth as student, professor, researcher, and scholar at the University of Chicago, a historically unique institution that fostered the creative and remarkably productive environment that was the Chicago School of Pragmatism. Among other things, Lasswell's association with this school meant that he was an early adopter of functionalism as a theoretical framework for his research on psychological, communications, political, and decision processes. Because Deweyan functionalism, beginning with his work on the reflex arc, involves teleological explanation, its adoption by Lasswell marks him as a member of the Aristotelian tradition of practical inference and, by extension, qualitative methodology. This tradition, when combined with the pragmatist principle of theory-practice unity, contributed to Lasswell's virtual mantra – "knowledge *of* and *in* the policy process" – and to continuous decision seminars and other institutional innovations. Indeed, given Lasswell's early experience and achievements at Chicago, especially his work with members of the "cross-disciplinary manifold," the policy sciences were a reality decades before their formal announcement in 1951.

Finally, when Lasswell described the policy sciences as "a contemporary adaptation of the general approach to public policy recommended by John Dewey and other pragmatists," he was not only giving credit to James, Peirce, Dewey, and colleagues at Chicago. He was also calling for the rediscovery of pragmatism as the origin of the policy sciences.

References

Ackoff, R. L. (1974a). Beyond Problem Solving. *General Systems*, 19, pp. 237–239.

Ackoff, R. L. (1974b). *Redesigning the Future: A Systems Approach to Societal Problems*. New York, NY: John Wiley.

Adelstein, R. (1992). Charles E. Lindblom. Division II Faculty Publications. Paper 92. Available at: http://wesscholar.wesleyan.edu/div2facpubs/92.

Adler, M. J. (1977). *Philosopher at Large: An Intellectual Autobiography.* Chicago, IL: University of Chicago Press.

Almond, G. A. (1987). *Harold Dwight Lasswell, 1902–1978: A Biographical Memoir.* Washington, DC: National Academy Press.

Almond, G. A. (2004). Who Lost the Chicago School of Political Science? *Perspectives on Politics*, 2(1), pp. 91–93.

Anderson, J. A. (2011). *Public Policymaking: An Introduction*. Boston, MA: Wadsworth.

Ansell, C. K. (2011). *Pragmatist Democracy: Evolutionary Learning As Public Philosophy.* New York, NY: Oxford University Press.

Arnold, T. (1937). *The Folklore of Capitalism*. New Haven, CT: Yale University Press.

Ascher, W. (1978). *Forecasting: An Appraisal for Policy-Makers and Planners*. Baltimore, MD: Johns Hopkins University Press.

Ascher, W. and Hirschfelder-Ascher, B. (2004). *Revitalizing Political Psychology: The Legacy of Harold D. Lasswell*. Chicago, IL: Psychology Press.

Atkins, W. E. and Lasswell, H. D. (1924). *Labor Attitudes and Problems*. Englewood Cliffs, NJ: Prentice-Hall.

Auer, M. R. (2007). The Policy Sciences in Critical Perspective. In J. Rabin, W. B. Hildreth, G. J. Miller, and J. Rabin, eds., *Handbook of Public Administration*, 3rd edn. Boca Raton, FL: CRC Press, Taylor & Francis, pp. 541–562.

Barnard, C. I. (1938). *The Functions of the Executive*. Cambridge, MA: Harvard University Press.

Bimber, B. (1998). The Death of an Agency: OTA and Trophy Hunting in US Budget Policy. *Policy Studies Review*, 15(2–3), pp. 202–225.

Bower, J. L. (1968). Descriptive Decision Theory from the "Administrative" Viewpoint. In R. A. Bauer and K. J. Gergen, eds., *The Study of Policy Formation*. New York, NY: Free Press, chapter 3.

Boyer, J. W. (2015). *The University of Chicago: A History.* Chicago, IL: University of Chicago Press.

Braybrooke, D. and Lindblom, C. E. (1963). *A Strategy of Decision: Policy Evaluation As a Social Process*. New York, NY: Free Press of Glencoe.

Brewer, G. D. and DeLeon, P. (1983). *The Foundations of Policy Analysis.* Homewood, IL: Dorsey Press.

Bromley, D. W. (2006). *Sufficient Reason: Volitional Pragmatism and the Meaning of Economic Institutions*. Princeton, NJ: Princeton University Press.

Bromley, D. W. (2008). Volitional Pragmatism. *Ecological Economics*, 68(1), pp. 1–13.

Brown, S. R. (2002). Structural and Functional Information. *Policy Sciences*, 35 (3), pp. 285–304.

Brunner, R. D. (1991). The Policy Movement As a Policy Problem. *Policy Sciences*, 24(1), pp. 65–98.

Brunner, R. D. (1997). Introduction to the Policy Sciences. *Policy Sciences*, 30(4), pp. 191–215.

Bulmer, M. (1984). *The Chicago School of Sociology: Institutionalization, Diversity, and the Rise of Sociological Research.* Chicago, IL: University of Chicago Press.

Burgess, E. W. (1916). The Social Survey: A Field for Constructive Service by Departments of Sociology. *American Journal of Sociology*, 21(3), pp. 492–500.

Campbell, D. T. (1988). *Epistemology and Methodology for Social Science: Collected Papers*. E. Samuel Overman, ed., Chicago, IL: University of Chicago Press.

Campbell, D.T. and Stanley, J. (1963). *Experimental and Quasi-Experimental Designs for Research*. Chicago, IL: Rand McNally.

Carey, J. T. (1975). *Sociology & Public Affairs: The Chicago School.* Newbury Park, CA: Sage Publications.

Churchman, C. W. (1967). Guest Editorial: Wicked Problems. *Management Science* 14(4), pp. B141–B142.

Colebatch, H. K. (2002). *Policy*, 2nd edn. Buckingham: Open University Press.

Collingwood, R. G. (1940). *An Essay on Metaphysics*. Oxford: Clarendon Press.

Cook, T. D. and Campbell, D. T. (1979). *Quasi-Experimentation: Design and Analysis Issues for Field Settings*. Boston, MA: Houghton Mifflin.

Corbacıoğlu, S. (2008). Invisible University in Public Policy Analysis: Cognitive and Social Networks among Six Social Scientists. *Review of Public Administration*, 2(4), pp. 27–54.

Couch, M. B. (2011). Causal Role Theories of Functional Explanation. In J. Fieser and B. Dowden, eds., *Internet Encyclopedia of Philosophy: A Peer Reviewed Academic Resource*. Available at: https://philpapers.org/rec/COUCRT [Accessed June 28, 2016].

Coughlin, N. (1973). *Young John Dewey: An Essay in American Intellectual History*. Chicago, IL: University of Chicago Press.

Crick, B. (1959). *The American Science of Politics: Its Origins and Conditions*. Berkeley, CA: University of California Press.

DeLeon, P. (1988). *Advice and Consent: The Development of the Policy Sciences*. New York, NY: Russell Sage Foundation.

DeLeon, P. (1992). The Democratization of the Policy Sciences. *Public Administration Review*, 52(2), pp. 125–129.

DeLeon, P. (1994). Reinventing the Policy Sciences: Three Steps Back to the Future. *Policy Sciences*, 27(1), pp. 77–95.

DeLeon, P. (1999). The Stages Approach to the Policy Process: What Has It Done? Where Is It Going? In P. A. Sabatier, ed.,*Theories of the Policy Process*. Boulder, CO: Westview Press, pp. 19–32.

DeLeon, P. (2006). The Historical Roots of the Field. In M. Moran, M. Rein, and R. E. Dery, eds., *Problem Definition in Policy Analysis*. Lawrence, KS: University Press of Kansas.

Deutsch, K., Platt, J., and Senghaas (1970). *Major Advances in Social Science since 1900: An Analysis of Conditions and Effects of Creativity*. Washington, DC: American Association for the Advancement of Science.

Deutsch, K., Markovits, A., and Platt, J., eds. (1986). *Advances in the Social Sciences, 1900–1986*. Lanham, MD: University Press of America.

Dewey, J. (1896). The Reflex Arc Concept in Psychology. *The Psychological Review* 3(4), pp. 357–370.

Dewey, J., (1922). *Human Nature and Conduct*. Southern Illinois University Press.

Dewey, J. (1933/1991). *How We Think*. Amherst, MA: Prometheus.

Dewey, J. (1938/1982). *Logic: The Theory of Inquiry*. New York, NY: Irvington.

Dewey, J. and Bentley, A. (1949). *Knowing and the Known*. Boston, MA: Beacon Press.

Diesing, P. (1992). *How Does Social Science Work? Reflections on Practice*. Pittsburgh, PA: University of Pittsburgh Press.

Dunn, W. N. (1988). Forethoughts: The Disputed Paternity of Technological Innovation. *Knowledge in Society*, 1(2), pp. 3–6.

Dunn, W. N. (2018). *Public Policy Analysis*, 6th edn. New York, NY: Routledge.

Dzuback, M. A. (1991). *Robert M. Hutchins: Portrait of an Educator*. Chicago, IL: University of Chicago Press.

Easton, D. (1950). Harold Lasswell: Policy Scientist for a Democratic Society. *Journal of Politics*, 12(3), pp. 450–477.

Eulau, H. and Zlomke, S. (1999). Harold Lasswell's Legacy to Mainstream Political Science: A Neglected Agenda. *American Review of Political Science*, 2, pp. 75–89.

Falk, R. A., Higgins, R., Reisman, W., and Weston, B. (1998). Myres Smith McDougal (1906–1998). *American Journal of International Law*, 92(4), pp. 729–733.

Farr, J., Hacker, J. S., and Kazee, N. (2006). The Policy Scientist of Democracy: The Discipline of Harold D. Lasswell. *American Political Science Review*, 100(4), pp. 579–587.

Fayol, H. (1916/1949). *General and Industrial Management*. London: Pitman.

Fischer, F. and Miller, G.J. eds., (2006). *Handbook of Public Policy Analysis: Theory, Politics, and Methods*. CRC Press.

Garrison, J. (2009). Dewey's Constructivism: From the Reflex Arc Concept to Social Constructivism. In L. Hickman , S. Neubert and K. Reich eds., *John Dewey: Between Pragmatism and Constructivism*. New York, NY: Fordham University Press, pp. 84–105.

Gerring, J. (2010). Causal Mechanisms: Yes, But .... *Comparative Political Studies*, 43(11), pp. 1499–1526.

Goodspeed, T. W. (1916). *A History of the University of Chicago*. Chicago, IL: University of Chicago Press.

Gulick, L. and Urwick, L., eds. (1937). *Papers on the Science of Administration*. New York, NY: Institute of Public Administration.

Hausman, D. M. (1992). *The Inexact and Separate Science of Economics*. New York, NY: Cambridge University Press.

Hayek, F. (1945). The Use of Knowledge in Society." *American Economic Review*, 35(4), pp. 519–530.

Hempel, C. G. (1959). The Logic of Functional Analysis. In L. Gross, ed., *Symposium on Sociological Theory*. Evanston, IL: Harper and Row.

Hempel, C. G. (1965). *Aspects of Scientific Explanation*. New York, NY: Free Press.

Hickman, L., Neubert, S. and Reich, K. eds. (2009). *John Dewey: Between Pragmatism and Constructivism*. New York, NY: Fordham University Press.

Hoppe, R. (1999). Policy Analysis, Science and Politics: From "Speaking Truth to Power" to "Making Sense Together." *Science and Public Policy*, 26(3), pp. 201–210.

Imbens, G. and Rubin, D. (2015). *Causal Inference for Statistics, Social, and Biomedical Sciences: An Introduction*. Cambridge: Cambridge University Press.

James, W. (1890/1950). *The Principles of Psychology*. Mineola, NY: Dover Press.

James, W. (1907). *Pragmatism, a New Name for Some Old Ways of Thinking: Popular Lectures on Philosophy*. New York, NY: Longman, Green, and Company.

James, W. (1909/1995). *Pragmatism*. Mineola, NY: Dover Press.

Jann, W. and Wegrich, K. (2007). Theories of the Policy Cycle. In F. Fischer and G. J. Miller, eds., *Handbook of Public Policy Analysis*. New York, NY: Routledge, pp. 69–88.

Jenkins-Smith, H. C. and Sabatier, P. A. (1993). The Study of the Public Policy Process. In P. A. Sabatier and H. C. Jenkins-Smith, eds., *Policy Change and Learning: An Advocacy Coalition Approach*. Boulder, CO: Westview Press, pp. 1–19.

Jones, C. O. (1977). *An Introduction to the Study of Public Policy*, 2nd edn. North Scituate, MA: Duxbury Press.

Kagel, A. and Roth, A. (1995). *Handbook of Experimental Economics*. Princeton, NJ: Princeton University Press.

Kaplan, A. (1964). *The Conduct of Inquiry: Methodology for Behavioral Science*. San Francisco, CA: Chandler Publishing Company.

Karl, B. D. (1975). *Charles E. Merriam and the Study of Politics*. Chicago, IL: University of Chicago Press.

Lasswell, H. D. (1936). *Politics: Who Gets What, When, How*. New York, NY: P. Smith.

Lasswell, H. D. (1938). *Propaganda Technique in the World War*. New York, NY: P. Smith.

Lasswell, H. D. (1941). The Garrison State. *American Journal of Sociology*, 46(4), pp. 455–468.

Lasswell, H. D. (1943). Personal Policy Objectives. Memorandum, October 1.

Lasswell, H. D. (1948). The Structure and Function of Communication in Society. In L. Bryson, ed., *The Communication of Ideas*. New York, NY: Institute for Religious and Social Studies, pp. 215–228.

Lasswell, H. D. (1951). The Policy Orientation. In D. Lerner and H. D. Lasswell, eds., *The Policy Sciences: Recent Developments in Scope and Method*. Palo Alto, CA: Stanford University Press, pp. 3–15.

Lasswell, H. D. (1956a). *The Decision Process: Seven Categories of Functional Analysis*. Lanham, MD: Bureau of Governmental Research, College of Business and Public Administration, University of Maryland.

Lasswell, H. D. (1956b). The Political Science of Science: An Inquiry into the Possible Reconciliation of Mastery and Freedom. *American Political Science Review*, 50(4), pp. 961–979.

Lasswell, H. D. (1960). Technique of Decision Seminars. *Midwest Journal of Political Science*, 4(3), pp. 213–236.

Lasswell, H. D. (1965). *World Politics and Personal Insecurity*. New York, NY: Free Press.

Lasswell, H. D. (1971a). *The Cross-Disciplinary Manifold: The Chicago Prototype*. In A. Lepawsky and E. Buehrig, eds., *Search for World Order*. New York, NY: Appleton-Century Crofts, pp. 417–428.

Lasswell, H. D. (1971b). *A Pre-View of Policy Sciences*. New York, NY: American Elsevier.

Lasswell, H. D. and Kaplan, A. (1950). *Power and Society: A Framework for Political Inquiry*. New Haven, CT: Yale University Press.

Lasswell, H. D. and Leites, N. C. (1965). *Language of Politics: Studies in Quantitative Semantics*. Boston, MA: MIT Press.

Lasswell, H. D. and McDougal, M. S. (1943). Legal Education and Public Policy: Professional Training in the Public Interest. *Yale Law Journal*, 52 (2), pp. 203–295.

Lasswell, H. D. and McDougal, M. S. (1992). *Jurisprudence for a Free Society: Studies in Law, Science, and Policy*. 2 vols. New Haven, CT: New Haven Press/Martinus Nijhoff Publishers.

Lerner, D., ed. (1959). *The Human Meaning of the Social Sciences*. New York, NY: World Publishing Company.

Lerner, D. and Lasswell, H. D., eds. (1951). *The Policy Sciences*. Palo Alto, CA: Stanford University Press.

Levison, A. (1966). Knowledge and Society. *Inquiry*, 9(1–4), pp. 132–146.

Lindblom, C. E. (1965). *The Intelligence of Democracy: Decision Making through Mutual Adjustment*. New York, NY: Free Press.

Lindblom, C. E. (1991). *Inquiry and Change*. New Haven, CT: Yale University Press.

Lindblom, C. E. and Cohen, D. K. (1979). *Usable Knowledge: Social Science and Social Problem Solving*. New Haven, CT: Yale University Press.

Lynd, R. S. (1939). *Knowledge for What? The Place of Social Science in American Culture*. Princeton, NJ: Princeton University Press.

Marshall, A., (1890). *Principles of Economics*. London, Macmillan.

May, J. V. and Wildavsky, A., eds. (1979). *The Policy Cycle*. Beverley Hills, CA: Sage Publications.

McDougal, M. S., Lasswell, H. D., and Reisman, W. M. (1967). The World Constitutive Process of Authoritative Decision. *Journal of Legal Education*, 19(3), pp. 253–230.

McDougal, M. S., Lasswell, H. D., and Reisman, W. M. (1972). The Intelligence Function and World Public Order. *Temple Law Quarterly*, 46, p. 365.

Menand, L., ed. (1997). *Pragmatism: A Reader*. New York, NY: Vintage.

Menand. L. (2001). *The Metaphysical Club*. New York, NY: Farrar, Straus, and Giroux.

Mitroff, I. I. (1974). *The Subjective Side of Science: A Philosophical Inquiry into the Psychology of the Apollo Moon Scientists*. Amsterdam: Elsevier Scientific.

Moore, A. W. (1910). *Pragmatism and Its Critics*. Chicago, IL: University of Chicago Press.

Nagel, E. (1968). *The Structure of Science: Problems in the Logic of Scientific Explanation*. New York, NY: Routledge and Kegan Paul.

Nakamura, R. T. (1987). The Textbook Policy Process and Implementation Research. *Review of Policy Research*, 7(1), 142–154.

National Academy of Sciences (2009). *The Use of Scientific Evidence in Public Policy*. Washington, DC: National Academies Press.

Parsons, T. (1949). *The Structure of Social Action*. New York, NY: Free Press.

Peirce, C. S. (1877). The Fixation of Belief. *Popular Science Monthly*, 12 (November).

Peters, B. G. and Pierre, J. (2016). *Comparative Governance: Rediscovering the Functional Dimension of Governing*. Cambridge: Cambridge University Press.

Peters J. D. and Simonson, P. (2004). *Mass Communication and American Social Thought: Key Texts, 1919–1968*. New York, NY: Addison-Wesley.

Polsby, N. W., Dentler, R. A., and Smith, P. A. (1963). *Politics and Social Life: An Introduction to Political Behavior*. Boston, MA: Houghton Mifflin.

Quade, E. S. (1989). *Analysis for Public Decisions*. 3rd rev. edn., G. M. Carter, ed. New York, NY: North Holland.

Raiffa, H., (1968). *Decision Analysis*. Reading, MA: Addison-Wesley.

Rein, M. and White, S. (1977). Policy research: Belief and doubt. *Policy Analysis*, 4(3), pp. 239–271.

Reisman, W. M. (1998). Theory about Law: Jurisprudence for a Free Society. *Yale Law Journal*, 108, pp. 935–937.

Rescher, N. (1977). *Methodological Pragmatism*. Oxford: Basil Blackwell.

Rescher, N. (1980). *Induction: An Essay on the Justification of Inductive Reasoning*. Pittsburgh, PA: University of Pittsburgh Press.

Rescher, N. (1995). Pragmatism. In T. Honderich, ed. *The Oxford Companion to Philosophy*. Oxford and New York, NY: Oxford University Press, pp. 710–714.

Rice, S. and Lasswell, H. D., eds. (1931). *Methods in the Social Sciences: A Case Book.* Chicago, IL: University of Chicago Press.

Rorty, R. (1999). Truth without Correspondence to Reality. In R. Rorty, *Philosophy and Social Hope*. Baltimore, MD: Penguin Books, pp. 23–46.

Rucker, D. (1969). *The Chicago Pragmatists: Dewey, Ames, Angell, Mead, Tufts, Moore*. Minneapolis, MN: University of Minnesota Press.

Sabatier, P. A. (1987). Knowledge, Policy-Oriented Learning, and Policy Change: An Advocacy Coalition Framework. *Science Communication*, 8(4), pp. 649–692.

Sabatier, P. A. (1988). An Advocacy Coalition Framework of Policy Change and the Role of Policy-Oriented Learning Therein. *Policy Sciences*, 21(2–3), pp. 129–168.

Sabatier, P. A. (1991). Toward Better Theories of the Policy Process. *PS: Political Science and Politics* 24(June), pp. 147–156.

Sabatier, P. A. ed. (1999, 2006). *Theories of the Policy Process*. 1st and 2nd edn. Boulder, CO: Westview Press.

Sabatier, P. A. and Weible, C., eds. (2014). *Theories of the Policy Process*. 3rd edn. Boulder, CO: Westview Press.

Salmon, W. C. (1984). *Scientific Explanation and the Causal Structure of the World*. Princeton, NJ: Princeton University Press.

Schickore, J. and Steinle, F., eds. (2006). *Revisiting Discovery and Justification: Historical and Philosophical Perspectives on the Context Distinction*, Vol. 14. New York, NY: Springer Science & Business Media.

Shadish, W., Cook, T. D., and Campbell, D. T. (2002). *Experimental and Quasi-Experimental Designs for Generalized Causal Inference*. Chicago, IL: Houghton Mifflin.

Shields, P. (2004). Classical Pragmatism: Engaging Practitioner Experience. *Administration & Society*, 36(3), pp. 351–361.

Shook, J. R. and Backe, A. (2001). *The Chicago School of Functionalism*. 3 vols. Bristol, UK: Thoemmes Press.

Simon, H. A. (1944). Decision-Making and Administrative Organization. *Public Administration Review*, 4(1), pp. 16–30.

Simon, H. A. (1947). *Administrative Behavior: A Study of Decision Making Processes in Administrative Organizations*. New York, NY: Macmillan.

Simon, H. A. (1973).The Structure of Ill Structured Problems. *Artificial Intelligence*, 4(3–4), pp. 181–201.

Storr, R. J. (1966). *A History of the University of Chicago: Harper's University – The Beginnings*. Chicago, IL: University of Chicago Press.

Tomas, V., ed. (1957). *Charles S. Peirce: Essays in the Philosophy of Science*. Edited with an introduction by Vincent Tomas. New York, NY: Liberal Arts Press.

Torgerson, D. (1985). Contextual Orientation in Policy Analysis: The Contribution of Harold D. Lasswell. *Policy Sciences*, 18(3), pp. 241–261.

Tribe, L. H. (1972). Policy Science: Analysis or Ideology? *Philosophy and Public Affairs*, 2(Fall), pp. 66–110.

Van Doren, J. and Roederer, C. J. (2012). McDougal-Lasswell Policy Science: Death and Transfiguration. *Richmond Journal of Global Law and Business*, 11(2), pp. 125–157.

Von Wright, G. H. (1971). *Explanation and Understanding*. Ithaca, NY: Cornell University Press.

Wagner, P., Weiss, C. H., Wittrock, B., and Wollman, H. (1994/2008). *Social Science and Modern States*. Cambridge: Cambridge University Press.

Webb, E. J., Campbell, D. T., Schwartz, R. D., and Sechrest, L. (1966). *Unobtrusive Measures: Nonreactive Research in the Social Sciences* (Vol. 111). Chicago, IL: Rand McNally.

Webber, M. M. and Rittel, H. W. (1974). Dilemmas in a General Theory of Planning. *Policy Sciences*, 4(2), pp. 155–169.

Weimer, D. and Vining, A. (2015). *Policy Analysis: Concepts and Practice*, 5th edn. New York, NY: Routledge.

Yale Law School Legal Scholarship Repository (1973). “Myres S. McDougal.” New Haven, CT.

Acknowledgments

The research reported here was informed by several prior efforts to investigate the relation between pragmatism, Lasswell, and the policy sciences. These prior efforts include "Rediscovering Pragmatism and the Policy Sciences," *European Policy Analysis*, 5(1) (May 2018); "The Policymaking Process: Lasswell's Unfinished Revolution," in Hoppe and Colebatch, eds., *Handbook of the Policy Process* (New York, NY: Edward Elgar, 2019); "Harold D. Lasswell and the Study of Public Policy," in Guy Peters, ed., *Oxford Research Encyclopedia of Politics* (London and New York, NY: Oxford University Press, 2018). These publications provided background materials and ideas for the present study.

At several phases in the development of this Element, the following persons provided help of different kinds. B. Guy Peters provided suggestions about the overall contours and purposes of this research, while M. Ramesh helped guide the manuscript through several twists and turns. Louise Comfort helped me understand the context at Yale when Lasswell and McDougal were active. Jeremy Weber and Ilia Murtazashvili provided insights into principles of pragmatism as they have been applied in one of the most systematic and original studies of pragmatism, economic institutions, and public policy, *Sufficient Reason: Volitional Pragmatism and the Meaning of Economic Institutions* (2006), by Daniel Bromley. In this context, I have also learned much over the years from the works of my colleague, Nicholas Rescher, including *Induction* (1980) and *Methodological Pragmatism* (1977). The late Alexander Weilenman sparked my interest in the Lasswell-McDougal project many years ago.

The history of the social sciences and philosophy at the University of Chicago figured prominently in this research, and my colleague Ryan Grauer has been important as a source and interpreter of historical works on the university. Rob Hoppe and Buzz Fozouni, as usual, are formidable critics who have continued over the years to induce reflective thinking in areas of the philosophy and sociology of science. Nick Turnbull provided initial reactions to this project that proved useful along the way. I am also grateful to an anonymous reviewer who convinced me to qualify several statements.

Early on, Rachel Travis helped compile all of John Dewey's collected works, although constraints on the length of the manuscript did not permit full and appropriate use of Dewey's works on education, public opinion, and democracy. Kelly Wadsworth assisted in the management of the many citations, as did Jessi Hanson. Marianne Dunn helped with unexpected technical tasks and, as always, was a quiet source of positive energy.

About the Author

William N. Dunn is Professor of Public Policy in the Graduate School of Public and International Affairs, University of Pittsburgh. His most well-known publication is *Public Policy Analysis: An Integrated Approach* (Routledge 2018), which is in its sixth edition and has been translated into six languages. He is a Russian and East European expert with long experience in the former Yugoslavia. His awards include the Donald T. Campbell and Douglas M. McGregor awards and the University of Pittsburgh Provost award for Excellence in Mentoring. He is an elected fellow of the National Academy of Public Administration.

Cambridge Elements

Public Policy

David L. Weimer

University of Wisconsin-Madison

David L. Weimer is the Edwin E. Witte Professor of Political Economy, University of Wisconsin-Madison. He has a long-standing interest in policy craft and has conducted policy research in the areas of energy, criminal justice, and health policy. In 2013 he served as president of the Society for Benefit-Cost Analysis. He is a Fellow of the National Academy of Public Administration.

About the Series

This series is a collection of assessments in the future of public policy research as well as substantive new research.

Edited by leading scholars in the field, the series is an ideal medium for reflecting on and advancing the understanding of critical issues in the public sphere. Collectively, the series provides a forum for broad and diverse coverage of all major topics in the field while integrating different disciplinary and methodological approaches.

Cambridge Elements

Public Policy

Elements in the Series

Designing for Policy Effectiveness: Defining and Understanding a Concept
B. Guy Peters, Giliberto Capano, Michael Howlett, Ishani Mukherjee, Meng-Hsuan Chou and Pauline Ravient

Making Policy in a Complex World
Paul Cairney, Tanya Heikkila and Matthew Wood

Pragmatism and the Origins of the Policy Sciences: Rediscovering Lasswell and the Chicago School
William N. Dunn

A full series listing is available at: www.cambridge.org/EPPO

Printed in the United States
By Bookmasters